WOMEN'S VOICES
FROM WEST AFRICA

WOMEN'S VOICES *from* WEST AFRICA

An Anthology of Songs from the Sahel

Edited by
**AISSATA G. SIDIKOU AND
THOMAS A. HALE**

Indiana University Press
BLOOMINGTON AND INDIANAPOLIS

This book is a publication of

Indiana University Press
601 North Morton Street
Bloomington, Indiana 47404-3797 USA

iupress.indiana.edu

Telephone orders   800-842-6796
Fax orders   812-855-7931

Library of Congress Cataloging-in-
Publication Data

Women's voices from West Africa : an
anthology of songs from the Sahel / edited by
Aïssata G. Sidikou and Thomas A. Hale.
   p. cm.
   Includes bibliographical references and
index.
   ISBN 978-0-253-35670-3 (cloth : alk. paper)
1. African poetry—Women authors. 2. African
poetry—Africa, West. 3. Oral tradition—
Africa, West. 4. Women in literature. 5.
Women—Africa, West—Social conditions.
I. Sidikou, Aïssata G. II. Hale, Thomas A.
(Thomas Albert), [date]
   PL8013.E5W66 2012
   808.8192870966—dc23

                                    2011029048

      1 2 3 4 5 17 16 15 14 13 12

We dedicate this book to the countless African women who express their hopes, loves, concerns, and views via the lyrics of their songs.

We also want to remember here the lives and contributions of two members of the Women's Songs research team who did not live to see the outcomes of this project: Louise Bourgault and Ariane Deluz.

Weyboro wangu si kafana; a ga zaama no
(Women's war never misses its goal;
they are always victorious)

—Songhoy-Zarma proverb

Contents

Preface and Acknowledgments

With this anthology, we bring song lyrics by African women to a wider public thanks to the help of a team of scholars from Africa, Europe, and North America. This project stems from our own research on women's songs over the last two decades.

In the 1990s, Aissata Sidikou recorded a variety of songs by women in Niger, including epics, a genre that is still the source of much debate because of diverse definitions and the view that in Africa this form appears to be limited to male narrators. The song lyrics appeared in *Recreating Words, Reshaping Worlds: The Verbal Art of Women from Niger, Mali and Senegal* (2001). A few years earlier, Thomas Hale, who had been conducting research on griots, realized that he needed to include women griots, or griottes, in his study in order to give a more complete picture of the profession. He interviewed scores of griottes in Niger, Mali, Senegal, and the Gambia and also recorded some songs for his book *Griots and Griottes: Masters of Words and Music* (1998).

In the course of our research, we began to encounter other scholars, primarily outside the field of African literature, who were also interested in women's songs. From these contacts, we began in the late 1990s to assemble a team of colleagues in anthropology, folklore, ethnomusicology, religion, and linguistics as well as literature: Louise Bourgault, Brahima Camara, Ariane Deluz, Bah Diakité, Marame Gueye, Jan Jansen, Marloes Janson, George Joseph, Charles Katy, Kirsten Langeveld, Beverly Mack, Fatima Mounkaïla, Nienke Muurling, Boubé Namaiwa, Aissata Niandou, Luciana Penna-Diaw, Susan Rasmussen, and Aline Tauzin. Some of them participated early in the project, while others have contributed songs more recently. Each had collected songs as part of a larger research project on a single ethnic group in the Sahel and in nearby areas of West Africa. Our initial research suggested that women were often expressing similar views through song across the ethnically diverse peoples of the region, but we wanted to confirm our findings with a much larger corpus, which our colleagues could provide.

With the support of a National Endowment for the Humanities collaborative research grant, our team began in 2001 to reexamine existing collections of recordings, some decades old; return to West Africa for follow-up or new field research; and comb archives for traces of song lyrics recorded by hand in the past. We invited the team members to meet at the Conference on Women's Songs from West Africa, held at Princeton University, May 2–4, 2003, to present the results of their research. Their efforts, as well as those of other researchers from the early twentieth century to the present, are at the heart of this anthology. Another outcome of the research by the scholars who presented papers at the Princeton conference, and others who could not attend or who have since contributed essays on their work, is a collection of papers that will appear as a companion volume. The two books are complementary, with the anthology providing a broad sampling of lyrics for regional comparisons and the essays offering deeper background on particular song traditions.

We want to thank all those who contributed to this project, including Elizabeth Arndt, our program officer at the National Endowment for the Humanities; the members of the research team; the many units at Princeton and at Penn State that provided support in various ways, from funding for the conference to sabbatical leaves for Aissata G. Sidikou and Thomas A. Hale; and Aaron Rosenberg, at the time a graduate student in comparative literature at Penn State, who organized files, scanned song lyrics, and in so many other ways helped us to prepare this volume.

All maps were created by the Gould Center for Geography Education and Outreach, Pennsylvania State University.

We view this anthology as the beginning of a larger project, one that will be carried forward not simply by the team with which we are currently working, but also by new generations of researchers who will help to widen and deepen our understanding of song as a vibrant form of verbal expression in Africa. We hope that our colleagues in many different disciplines will find this collection useful for both instruction and research on verbal art in West Africa.

Aissata G. Sidikou
Thomas A. Hale

*   *   *

The editors gratefully acknowledge the kindness of the following publishers and one individual for granting permission to reprint previously published materials and one unpublished text.

"If your mother-in-law scolds you," "Fulle has arrived," "Fat is Gold," and "Now she took the calabash of millet" from *Recreating Worlds: the Verbal Art of Women from Mali, Niger, and Senegal* (2001) by Aissata G. Sidikou, reproduced by permission of Africa World Press.

"My sisters" and "I remember the day" from *Poetry, Prose, and Popular Culture in Hausa* (1996) by Graham Furniss, reproduced by permission from Edinburgh University Press.

"La petite Ayira a crié," "Mon père et ma mère, je vous l'ai dit," "Ceci n'est pas un refus," "La femme d'un vieux," "L'enfant qu'on met au monde," "Reconduis-moi chez ma mère," "Papa commandant," "Les hommes de maintenant," and "Ho, appelez les femmes" from *Chants de Femmes au Mali* (1981, 2010) by René Luneau; "Le mari qui est venu nous voir" in *Figures du féminin dans la société maure* (2001) by Aline Tauzin, reproduced by permission of Editions Karthala.

"O Ginaan, fille de Yande" in *La femme Seereer (Sénégal)* (2005) by Issa Thiaw; "Nous implorons le secours d'Allah," "S'il y avait un peu d'ombre," "Un enfant a vu le jour," and "Le jour de notre marriage est arrivé" in *Chants traditionnels du pays Soninke* (1990) by Moussa Diagana; "Narre Yamma" and "Provocation" in *Les Oiseaux s'ébattent: Chansons enfantines de Burkina Faso* (1993) by Kabore Oger, reproduced by permission from Editions L'Harmattan.

"O Fanta" in "Song, Performance and Power: The Bèn Ka Di Women's Association in Bamako" by Kate Modic, Diss., Indiana University, 1996.

"From What Ruby" in *Shinqiti Folk Literature and Song* (1968) by H. T. Norris, by permission of Oxford University Press.

"Fatou J" and "I Say, Abdou Diouf" in *Selfish Gifts: Senegalese Women's Autobiographical Discourses* (2001) by Lisa McNee, reproduced with permission by SUNY Press.

WOMEN'S VOICES
FROM WEST AFRICA

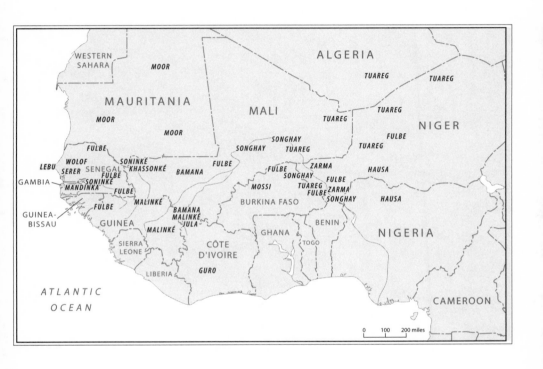

⟶ᴄᴏ *Introduction*

THE POWERFUL VOICES OF WOMEN IN SONG

In the novel *L'Aventure ambiguë* (Ambiguous Adventure, 1961) by Cheikh Hamidou Kane, an unusually powerful Fulbe princess, the Most Royal Lady, calls for a meeting of the town's inhabitants in order to examine collectively the question of whether to send the children of their Diallobé clan to the French colonial school. She salutes her mixed audience in the public square by explaining the exceptional nature of this event: "I have done something which is not pleasing to us and which is not in accordance with our customs. I have asked the women to come to this meeting today. We Diallobé hate that, and rightly, for we think that the women should remain at home" (45). Her public acknowledgment of the widespread view that women's place is in the home serves to underscore the exceptional nature of the meeting she has called. At the same time, her role as the convener and leader of the meeting contradicts the stereotype of the voiceless African woman. For some readers who are discovering African literature, the speech by the Most Royal Lady comes as a great surprise: she does not fit the image they have of women in Africa.

Although it is difficult to generalize from the example of a single people in a continent as vast and diverse as Africa, the Diallobé of northern Senegal have many values similar to those of other groups in the Sahel region. The Diallobé are part of a dispersed and varied group of peoples known as Fulbe, Fulani, or Peul. Among the earliest to embrace Islam nearly a millennium ago, they also share with many other peoples in the region a social structure that is marked by patriarchy and polygyny. From the outside, women's place appears indeed to be limited to the domestic sphere, as the Most Royal Lady suggests, while men dominate the public space. But the reality is more complex, and one cannot grasp the subtleties of gender roles unless one understands the meaning and force of women's views. If public speaking to a mixed audience constitutes an exception to tradition, there is another medium of expression that women employ every day and with great freedom: song.

The song is a medium of entertainment that conjures up memories of gentle genres such as the lullaby. In this volume, however, one will find not only lullabies but also a collection of rather direct and in a few cases shocking songs, some of which inspire fear in men. Many of these songs come from the vast corpus devoted to marriage, an institution that affects women in many ways, and they oblige us to rethink any notion that women lack a voice in Sahelian societies.

African women express their diverse views about marriage in song lyrics that are often quite astonishing to those who see them as voiceless victims. In examples from across the region, we find women threatening to commit suicide if they are forced to marry someone they do not love. A wife who must receive a second wife in the home is supported by friends who hurl ritual insults at the new arrival. In one example from Niger, women threaten to sabotage the marriage by rubbing hot pepper on the testicles of the husband. In another from Senegal, the friends of the first wife insult the new arrival by asking, "Doesn't the bride have friends? / She has only one bundle and her ass / Looks like a seasonal worker to me!" Finally, if after settling into the husband's home a new bride suffers abuse from other wives or members of the husband's family, the lyrics of songs declare that "leaving home is not a crime."

VERBAL ART AND SONG

These insulting songs shatter any notion that women are too shy to express themselves in verbal art in a public context. By *verbal art,* we mean all forms that are written and spoken. Narrative in oral forms stretches back for tens of thousands of years, and Africans have been writing in African languages for at least five thousand years. During the twentieth century, African writers, first men and then women, began producing novels, plays, and poetry in European languages. But these relatively recent written forms represent a small fraction of a much larger and more complex array of verbal art that includes oral epics, stories, poems, proverbs, riddles, sayings, and songs heard in villages, towns, and cities across Africa. They are heard live and on recordings played for small groups and broadcast on the radio. In that diverse soundscape, women feature prominently.

But even as a form of verbal art, songs are nearly invisible in the work of scholars interested in African literature, a field focused to a large extent on contemporary fiction in English or French. For example, if one examines the programs for the annual meetings of the African Literature Association since the organization was founded in 1974, the study of narratives or poetry recorded from oral sources constitutes an infinitesimal part of the research of the members. At best, one finds an occasional paper on the oral epic, a lengthy genre that has attracted the attention of a small but growing group of researchers.

There are many reasons for this lack of literary interest in songs. First, the lyrics are rarely translated by those who know the song's language. Second, there are approximately 1,500 languages in Africa (the number depends on where one draws the line between language and dialect). It is rare to find anyone who can master more than a few of them. Third, many scholars in African literature from Europe and North America who trained in departments of English or French do not know any African languages. Fourth, where there is room for a translated exemplar of the oral tradition in a syllabus, the choice will likely be an epic in reconstructed prose rather than a song or some other short form. A final reason may be a belief that songs are so embedded in the local context that they do not have wide significance in the diverse world of verbal art.

In spite of this lack of interest on the part of many African literature scholars, a generation of researchers from folklore, anthropology, communications, ethnomusicology, and other disciplines, as well as literature, has begun to explore the world of women's songs. Well before the publication of our own books, mentioned in the preface, René Luneau had collected songs by women as a medium for understanding society in "Les Chemins de la Noce" (The Pathways to Marriage), a 1974 dissertation that led to a collection titled *Chants de femmes au Mali* (1981, 2010). It was followed by Pascal Couloubaly's *Une société rurale bambara à travers des chants de femmes* (1990). Beverly Mack's three decades of study of Hausa women's oral and written poetry, including *Muslim Women Sing* (2004), reveal the fluidity of the relationship between the oral performances and written compositions she collected in Kano, Nigeria. Lucy Durán has been documenting for several decades the growth of popular song in West Africa in a long series of articles, chapters, and liner notes, including her 1999 dissertation, "Stars and Songbirds: Mande Female Singers in Urban Music, Mali 1980–1999." Lisa McNee published *Selfish Gifts: Senegalese Women's Autobiographical Discourses* (2000), a study that reveals the diversity of Wolof women's verbal art as a form of self-representation. Marloes Janson, in *The Best Hand Is the Hand That Always Gives* (2002), offers insights into both professional and nonprofessional women singers in the Gambia. Louise Bourgault explores the role of songs by both men and women in fighting AIDS in *Playing for Life: Performance in Africa in the Age of AIDS* (2003). South of the Sahel, other scholars have included songs by women in studies of music, notably Ruth Stone in *Let the Inside Be Sweet* (1982), an ethnography of the music of the Kpelle in Liberia, and Karin Barber in *I Could Speak till Tomorrow: Oriki, Women, and the Past in a Yoruba Town* (1991), a study of a particular genre of Yoruba song performed by both women and men.

A REGIONAL APPROACH

The Sahel, the focus of this project, is a region with long-standing and closely linked cultural roots, what Paul Stoller has termed deep Sahelian civilization (Hale and Stoller 1985). The peoples share a common history in the rise and fall of overlapping empires and kingdoms from the tenth century to the sixteenth century (Ghana, Mali, and Songhoy) and in the creation of a variety of other states in the years since then (for example, Wolof in Senegal, Segou in Mali, and Sokoto in Nigeria). They also share a variety of common social structures that are hierarchical and patriarchal, customs that include polygyny and guilds of artisans such as blacksmiths, leatherworkers, carvers, and griots.

By taking this regional approach, we do not intend to undercut the importance of the local context as the key to the deep meaning of a song. The researchers who have contributed songs to this volume have recorded and analyzed the lyrics in a way that allows the greatest opportunity to grasp the full meaning of each performance. A forthcoming companion volume will include research narratives from some of these scholars, and we have included some of their representative work in the bibliography.

When one steps back from the microtext of a particular song in order to compare, for example, the lyrics of singers from Senegal, Mali, and Niger all complaining about polygyny, the warp and woof of those verbal threads reveal a regional fabric that complements the local perspective. In this anthology, we will provide some examples from this and other categories to illustrate the cultural continuity across the Sahel. There are so many different types of songs for each occasion, for example, songs on the departure of the bride from her home, that we do not always have space to include multiple examples from each category. Nevertheless, the variety of our subjects, combined with several instances of more common topics, such as the decision to marry, will provide a broad tapestry that supports our two points: there are common themes across the region, and there is great diversity in the kinds of songs that women sing.

WOMEN SINGERS IN HISTORICAL CONTEXT

If we now know more about song in the Sahel today thanks to the research of a growing corps of scholars interested in the genre, it is not because women have just begun to sing. Evidence for women singing in Africa may be found as early as the ancient Egyptians. One finds a wide range of verbal and visual evidence that women sang for a variety of occasions. For example, in *Music and Musicians in Ancient Egypt* (1991), Lisa Manniche offers numerous reproductions of images of women singing and performing on instruments as well as the lyrics of songs about gods and goddesses, men and women. In *Love Songs of the New*

Kingdom (1974), edited and translated by Jack Foster, one finds in "I Found My Love by the Secret Canal" sensuous lyrics about a relationship that dates to the time of the nineteenth and twentieth dynasties, around 1300 bCE:

> I found my love by the secret canal,
> Feet dangling down in the water
> He had made a hushed cell in the thicket for worship
> To dedicate to this day.
> To holy elevation of the flesh.
> He brings light to what is hidden.
> (breast and thigh go bare, go bare),
> Now, raised on high toward his altar, exalted
> Ah! . . .
> A tall man is more than his shoulders! (11)

From the verse points rendered in red at the end of each line in the original as well as from a variety of other evidence, Egyptologists have concluded that this text is the transcription of a song by a female singer, or *shemayt*.

The song confirms the existence of an activity that was practiced all over the continent at the time. In 1352–1353 CE, nearly three thousand years later, an Amazigh (or Berber) traveler from Tangiers, Ibn Battuta, encountered women singers at the court of Mali. He described the women as a choral backup to Dugha, the chief *jali*, or griot, of Mansa Suleyman. On Muslim holy days when the ruler holds court, the author recounted, Dugha narrates the story of the deeds of his master while accompanied by "his four wives and [his] concubines, who are about a hundred in number." Dugha plays an instrument and speaks while "the wives and concubines sing along with him and they play with bows" (Hamdun and King 1975:41–42). From this description, it is clear that the *jalimusolu*, or female griots, of the Mande peoples in Mali were part of the elite at the court of this ruler. In this case, they played an important role in the celebration of the deeds of Mansa Suleyman on a holy day.

Ibn Battuta's description provides something of a benchmark for references by other writers. In the seventeenth century, the Timbuktu chronicles that describe the Ghana, Mali, and Songhoy empires, the *Tarîkh el-Fettâch* (Kâti 1981) and the *Tarîkh es-Sudan* (Es-Sa'di 1964), include references to women singers. Much of the description in these long narratives focuses on the Songhoy empire from the late fifteenth century through the sixteenth and early seventeenth. As Hunwick pointed out in the introduction to his more recent English translation of the latter narrative, the court of Songhoy was similar to that of Mali, with Songhoy *jeserey*, or griots, as spokespersons accompanied by women. The narrator of the *Tarîkh es-Sudan* describes how Askia Mohammed Bonkana, who had taken the Songhoy throne in 1531, following the regime of Askia Moussa, ordered a *jesere weyboro*, or griotte, Yana Mara, to declaim to him continually, in the presence of the daughters of Askia Mohammed, the following: "A single ostrich chick is better than a hundred hen chicks." The saying was meant to emphasize his importance as the son of Umar Komadiaka, brother of Askia Mohammed, in comparison with the children of Askia Moussa (126). The *jesere weyboro* was, in effect, the voice of the ruler at a time of regime change.

In these two references, the first from the fourteenth century and the second from the early seventeenth century, a common feature is that women singers played a role at court. Between then and the present, accounts by European writers offer numerous descriptions of performances—but no lyrics—by women singing in both royal and common contexts. The French trader Michel Jajolet de La Courbe, director of the Compagnie du Sénégal, based at the mouth of the Senegal River, encountered griottes singing on a variety of occasions near his post and during trips inland beginning in 1685. For example, in 1686 he described the singing of a *tiggiwit*, or Moor griotte, who accompanied the mother of Leydy, a ruler from north of the Senegal River. When she paid a visit to La Courbe at a stop along the river, the French trader noted that the performer accompanying her

> held a kind of twelve-stringed harp whose body was made of a calabash covered with leather which she played rather nicely. She began therefore to sing a fairly melodious Arab song, but rather languid, a little in the style of the Spanish or Portuguese, accompanying it with her harp with much restraint. But what was most agreeable was that she really threw herself into the performance by making all kinds of movements and gestures of her head, which made her gris-gris [talismans] and pendants shake, showing the most beautiful teeth in the world. (La Courbe 1913:172; cited in Hale 1998:91)

Nearly a century and a half later, René Caillé, the eccentric French traveler who was the first European to reach Timbuktu and return to tell about it, reported in 1830 the pleasure of listening to women singing in Bangoro, a small town on the road to Jenne in Mali, where he stopped in July 1827.

In the evening, women came to the market square, 100 of them. . . . Several held tambourines made out of a calabash covered with tanned sheepskin. . . . They sang savage tunes with a deep voice and jumped together in cadence while shaking their drums. . . . I saw . . . other women who had a drum hanging from their necks on the end of which was a little piece of wood covered with little bells and pieces of metal that shook and sounded at each movement. (Caillé 1989:vol. 2, 77; cited in Hale 1998:103)

Neither La Courbe nor Caillé understood what the women were saying in their songs. Their musical criticism reflected the many biases of Europeans about African peoples. But by the early twentieth century, as the French completed their conquest of a large swath of West Africa, colonial administrators began to take a keener interest in what their subjects were thinking, the better to strengthen the domination of France in the region. A striking example from early in the twentieth century reveals much about not only the performer, but also the collector. The context is sufficiently complex and the self-serving motives of the French in disseminating the song so evident that one must dig through several layers of meaning to arrive at what appear to be the true feelings of the singer. "Diossé Lost the Men Uselessly," sung by a woman who lost her only son in a rebellion against the French, combines both lamentation and criticism against African leaders. Given the woman's negative portrayal of her own leaders, it is not surprising that the song was of great interest for the French, who sought by any means to find support for the colonial enterprise. We have listed the song under "Lamentations about Children," but it might also have been included as an example of women's involvement in politics.

SONGS AS MODELS FOR ACTION

If the singer can be a fierce critic of her society, she can also keep the social fabric together by textualizing and historicizing events; announcing, answering, or accentuating concerns; and exploring the conditions of people in her songs. As a form of discourse, songs can provide or construct models for action and thought in the communities where they are heard. The medium is not limited to professional singers—any woman can sing, and her songs may serve as verbal spaces where taboos can be attacked; thought processes contrasted; feelings expressed, exposed, and filtered; stereotypes emphasized or rejected; and selves constructed or shattered. From this larger perspective, the songs in this collection serve as verbal mirrors of individuals, their daily lives, history, space, and the social dynamics governing a society. To sing is to make public, even though there are instances when young women might compose songs in anonymity in order to avoid censorship or punishment.

SONGS AS PERFORMANCE

Although we are acutely aware of the importance of performance and context in understanding the full meaning of a song, the focus in this collection is on the lyrics, the fundamental component of a song and the foundation for its content. In some communities women do not normally play musical instruments—for example, the twenty-one-stringed kora—and some songs require no more than the human voice. But others call for instruments that may range from an upside-down calabash floating in a basin of water to kitchen utensils, even a mortar and pestle. The use of instruments depends on the type of song and the occasion on which it is sung. Whatever the circumstances, with or without instruments, the members of the audience engage in a discourse of the imagination with the singer when they participate by singing, playing instruments, or dancing. Although it is impossible to convey the dynamics of a performance using only the transcribed and translated lyrics of a song, we plan to create a website that will offer original recordings of some of the songs.

THE MANY ROLES OF SONGS

Songs have multiple functions in society depending on the task, event, or ceremony that they accompany. Some are solemn, while others are cheerful. Some create a bridge between the singer and her community, while others are seductive or destructive. Some singers, especially the professionals, are rewarded for their performances, while others simply seek to communicate with their audiences with no expectation of reward.

Songs can be of ritual and esoteric nature but most are secular. Their focus may be political, historical, social, economic, medical, or environmental. They are composed on different occasions and their subjects can be as diverse as the songs themselves. Songs are usually sung for people, but they may also celebrate or reject animals, places, nature, objects, and organizations. Songs can establish ties between people or places, but they can also destroy relationships. Singers may praise people and their qualities, or they may abuse their subjects by pointing out their imperfections. One hears songs at almost every ceremony, including naming, initiation, and marriage.

Songs are a unifying aspect of West African societies but they may also be inaccessible at times, depending on the occasion. Some songs are ephemeral and occasional, while others tell about events and people of the distant past and have been handed down for centuries. Songs of initiation, for example, focus on the deeply rooted values that a society considers important for the formation of young adults.

Although songs may contribute to the influence of an individual, often through praise, they may also focus on the position of the weak, especially those who do not appear to exercise much power or influence in the community, especially women. The lyrics may engage controversial social issues by confronting all the members of society and pointing to the need to change beliefs and practices that govern the relationships between people. Songs may function as healing devices for the women who sing them, but they may also be harmful to those they expose.

Songs may be sung for a variety of purposes and events: lullabies to help put a child to sleep, initiations, expressions of love, tattooing, naming, wrestling, food preparation. But one activity dominates the songscape for women: marriage.

MARRIAGE SONGS

The collection of songs presented here demonstrates that beyond regional specificity there is a continuity when it comes to the institution of marriage. There are many reasons for this emphasis. First, marriage is often viewed as the most important event in a woman's life. Her social status is often seen as ambiguous until she marries and has children. Second, marriage is seen as the basis of a union not simply between two people but between families and clans. This political dimension of marriage emerges from the many examples of rulers who sought to confirm and strengthen relationships by marrying women from regions and states that they conquered or with which they wished to establish a closer tie. Finally, marriage is seen as the foundation on which a society is able to perpetuate itself. The ability of a society to nourish and defend itself depends on the replacement of old people with new generations.

But marriage involves disruption as a bride moves from one space, her family's home, to a new situation in which she may be seen in a positive manner as extending her family or be viewed as an outsider upsetting an established family dynamic. For this reason, many of the songs in this collection are devoted to the position of the young girl and the problems she may encounter in her new space. These concerns about the role and status of women appear in songs across the region.

The significance of marriage for women and the conditions that make it appear to weigh more on the woman than on the man have led to forms of song that soothe or address negative responses to the institution. The singers may describe the psychological scars that follow the displacement of the young bride, the impact of a hostile mother-in-law, brother-in-law, or sister-in-law on the bride, the consequences of living with an irresponsible husband, or the

disruption that may be created by a potential co-wife. Marriage songs also celebrate the young bride, but most of them seek to socialize the bride to embrace
the values that are the ideals of a society. In most cases, those ideals impact
more directly the lives of women than those of men.

Given the complexity of marriage as a cultural phenomenon, songs about
it reveal great thematic diversity: love and courtship, departure from home,
lamentation, adultery, advice to the bride, arranged marriages, May-December
relationships, sex, polygyny, sterility, abuse, rejection, and divorce. The songs
are rooted in a variety of ethno-specific genres, but the themes cut across the
entire region. Above all, they reveal that women enjoy a remarkable freedom to
speak out publicly through song lyrics about their relationships with men and
with others in society, such as relatives and co-wives. The contents of the songs
are not limited to women. Some refer to men and are quite graphic and shocking in their direct references to sex. These songs reveal a great deal of freedom
of expression on the part of the women who sing them.

SONG AND LITERATURE: MAIMOUNA'S SONG

The link between these songs, contemporary literature by African authors, and
politics may not be apparent unless one considers the extraordinary role of
women in one of the most powerful novels to come out of Francophone Africa,
Les bouts de bois de Dieu (God's Bits of Wood, 1960) by Ousmane Sembène. The
subject is a railroad strike that occurred in French West Africa in 1947, and in
particular the conflict between workers and management. Maimouna, a blind
beggar who plays a small but key role in the novel, sings songs that galvanize
her listeners at crucial moments in the narrative. During the opening battle
between strikers and the police at the railroad's headquarters in the city of
Thiès, Senegal, she sings about Goumba N'Diaye, a legendary heroine of the
past who demands a great deal of her suitor:

> "I have come to take a wife," the stranger said.
> "My bridegroom must be stronger than I.
> There are my father's fields,
> And there are the abandoned scythes,"
> replied Goumba N'Diaye.
> And the stranger took up a scythe.
> Two days each week, and still they came not to the end,
> But the man could not vanquish the girl. (21)

The song sets the tone for a conflict in which, indeed, the women demand
much of the men, take on new responsibilities themselves, and prod their part-

ners to stand up to the French. The song reflects Sembène's emphasis on the importance of verbal art. More important, it reveals a reverence for the role of women as performers and preservers of the oral tradition. Finally, the song underscores the novel's message of solidarity for both men and women. Toward the end of the novel, at a crucial moment when the hero, Bakayoko, speaks to a large crowd, the women "formed into a solid rank and were improvising words to a chant dedicated to their men."

> The morning light is in the east;
> It is daybreak of a day of history.
> From Koulikoro to Dakar
> The smoke of the savanna dies.
> On the 10th of October, fateful day,
> We swore before the world
> To support you to the end.
> You have lit the torch of hope,
> And victory is near.
> The morning is in the east;
> It is daybreak of a day of history. (172)

The songs in *Les bouts de bois de Dieu* remind us that while women benefited very little from Western-style education during the colonial era, they were not voiceless. But if we correctly understand the songs, thanks to the novelist's translation or recreation, it is clear from the context that the French administrators have no clue about what the women are saying in their lyrics and, in fact, are frightened by the presence of these singing protesters outside their offices. When the women begin to sing, the French negotiators become nervous. A young and rather naïve employee asks the older and more experienced administrators of the railroad, "Do you understand what the women are singing? It may have something to do with the strike." "Don't be a fool," Isnard (one of the administrators) snaps. "It is just shouting and yelling, as usual. What do you think they know about the strike? They're just making noise because they like to make noise" (172).

SONG, LITERACY, AND VERBAL ART

While songs represent a powerful form of female expression, one that cannot be excluded from our notion of what constitutes African literature, they also force us to reconsider another feature of contemporary African literary criticism: the tendency to view the subject from an evolutionary perspective. At one point in the development of the field of orality and literacy, some researchers concluded that the evolution of societies depended on a shift from one medium to the other. Other scholars argued that such a view constituted a reframing of the "primitive" versus "civilized" dichotomy that is said to distinguish the Western world from other regions. That view has become more nuanced since the 1980s as scholars have come to understand more clearly the complex connections between orality and literacy. Graham Furniss has provided an excellent summary of this relationship in "Orality versus Literacy: The Great Divide Debate," a section in chapter 5 of his study *Orality: The Power of the Spoken Word* (2004:131–141). Unfortunately, the evolutionary perspective still influences some researchers in African literature who view the late arrival of women on the literary scene as a form of advancement from the oral to the written.

Irène d'Almeida, Obioma Nnaemeka, Odile Cazenave, and others have underscored the fact that women were excluded from the literary scene in large part because Western-style education during the colonial and early national periods was provided in a more sustained fashion only to boys, with girls dropping out early as the result of marriage or the perceived need to devote family resources to those offspring who could succeed in a male-oriented world. By eventually acquiring literacy in spite of these limitations, women writers have managed to break the bonds of silence that surrounded them. From a wider perspective on verbal art that includes both oral and written forms, however, it is clear that women have always had a voice. The problem is that the voice was expressed in song and in languages not understood by those from other parts of Africa or from outside of Africa.

A more comprehensive way, then, of viewing the verbal art of women is to conclude that oral and written forms coexist today. Those women who have experienced Western-style education are now using the medium of writing in European languages to communicate to global audiences. They may nevertheless borrow here and there from oral sources for their narratives. Ken Bugul and Werewere Liking, for instance, offer many examples of this approach in their works. The majority of women in Africa, however, continue to express themselves through song. Such a dual approach reflects Brian Street's (1984) theory about the relationship between orality and literacy. The medium, oral or written, is not what counts. It is the language in which a message or an art form is composed that is of greatest importance because that language carries a significant load of cultural baggage.

This is well illustrated in a Sahelian capital such as Niamey, Niger, where people may greet each other and pray in Arabic, converse in Songhoy-Zarma or Hausa, and conduct business at the office in French. Arabic is both written and oral; Songhoy-Zarma and Hausa are mainly oral, but there are a few publications in Songhoy-Zarma and a much longer tradition of writing in Hausa; while

French, the colonial language, can serve for both oral and written purposes. What matters is the culture conveyed by these languages: Arabic bears a major religious tradition that arrived centuries ago; Songhoy-Zarma and Hausa each carry a much older heritage; French reflects the impact—and the constraints—of France's policies on the government, peoples, and ways of Niger in both the colonial and national eras. Orality and literacy are, then, secondary concerns when we consider what lies behind each language.

The evidence suggests that song is indeed a privileged medium of expression for women across the Sahel. If we are to understand fully the dimensions of a verbal art recorded from oral sources, then we can no longer ignore what women are saying in their songs. We hope that the lyrics included in this anthology will inspire instructors in African literature to make space in course reading lists for songs, a ubiquitous verbal form with the oldest heritage and the widest impact in Africa.

PEOPLES, LANGUAGES, AND MAPS

Nearly all of the peoples in this anthology share many common elements, but they have diverse histories and live in different parts of the Sahel and nearby regions. While the focus is on the common themes that link women, we offer below brief descriptions of many of the groups, and maps to situate them in the area covered by this anthology. Spellings generally follow American usage (e.g., Bamana instead of Bambara), with some exceptions. Other terms associated with each people, or group of related peoples speaking the same language, appear in parentheses below. The countries cited are where the majority lives, but in many cases smaller groups can be found in other parts of the region. The peoples include the Bamana (Bambara) of Mali; the Fulbe (Fula, Fulani, Peul, Toucouleur) of Senegal, Gambia, Guinea, Mali, and Niger; the Guro in Côte d'Ivoire; the Hausa in Nigeria and Niger; the Jula (Dyula, Dioula) in Mali, Guinea, and Côte d'Ivoire; the Khassonké in Mauritania and Mali; the Lebu (Lébou) in Senegal; the Malinké in Mali and Guinea; the Mandinka in Gambia and Senegal; the Moors (Maures) in Mauritania; the Mossi in Burkina Faso; the Serer in Senegal; the Songhoy (Songhay, Sonrai) in Mali and Niger; the Soninké in Mauritania, Senegal, Gambia, and Mali; the Tuareg (Touareg) in Mali and Niger; the Wolof in Senegal; and the Zarma (Zerma) in Niger and Mali.

The languages spoken in the region are often related to some degree. Linguists tend to define these relationships in terms of language versus dialect. But the distinction is subject to debate among both these specialists and the peoples themselves. Given both the ambiguity of the frontier between language and dialect, and the unfortunate tendency of those outside the continent to label all African languages as dialects, we will simply use the term *language* here for what is spoken by each of these peoples.

Below are maps and descriptions for most of the peoples whose songs are included in this collection.

Bamana

The Bamana (Bambara, Banmana) are one of many Mande peoples (Soninké, Khassonké, Mandinka, and Guro, for example). Their language, known as Bamanakan, is close to other Mande languages, and is spoken by 80 percent of the 14 million people in Mali today.

The roots of their dominance in Mali and surrounding areas go back several centuries. Migrating north from southern Mali and northern Côte d'Ivoire, they began to establish a powerful presence in the upper Niger region. They founded their first kingdom in 1640. In the nineteenth century, they formed the kingdoms of Ségou, Bélédougou, and Kaarta, but as they expanded their zone of influence, they came under attack by a variety of other peoples. They were conquered in 1861 by El Hadj Umar Tall, a powerful figure known for spreading Islam across the Sahel.

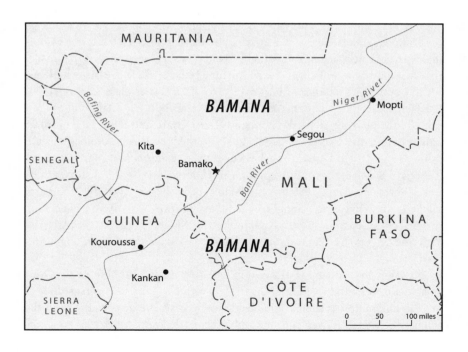

Although Islam continued to diffuse in the region throughout the nineteenth century, the Bamana resisted the new religion. Today, the vast majority of Bamana are Muslim, but many of them have maintained their traditional, pre-Islamic system of beliefs.

Bamana society is based on patrilineal descent, with a community leader chosen by elders. Traditional ways are disappearing with the migration of people to the cities, in particular to Mali's capital, Bamako, which has 2 million inhabitants. Of the many different ethnic groups in Mali today, Bamana play the most dominant role in government and other sectors of society. There are now over 6 million Bamana in Mali and in neighboring countries.

Fulbe

The Fulbe are called Fula by the Mandinka, Fulani by the Hausa, Fulan by the Songhoy-Zarma, and Peul by the Wolof. Their language, Fulfulde, is spoken across a wide swath of the Sahel. They are best known for their role in the spread of Islam throughout West Africa and for the creation of a series of empires and kingdoms, especially in the eighteenth and nineteenth centuries.

The Fulbe migrated throughout the Sahel region of West Africa and first settled in the Futa Toro area of northern Senegal. Originally pastoral nomads,

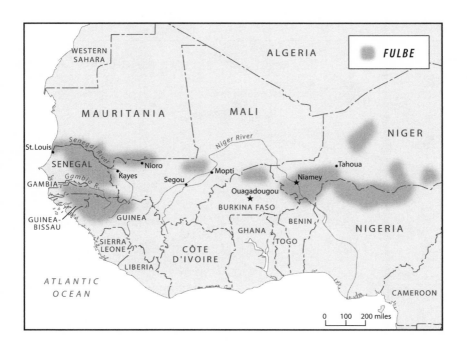

they scattered across a vast region that includes Mauritania, Senegal, Gambia, Mali, Chad, Guinea-Bissau, Sierra Leone, Liberia, Burkina Faso, Togo, Benin, Niger, Nigeria, Cameroon, and the Central African Republic. In spite of a population of 25 million people, the Fulbe remain a minority ethnic group in most countries, with the exception of Guinea where they constitute the most numerous people. Of the 10 million people in that country, 4 million are Fulbe. Although nearly half of Fulbe still live as nomads, today more and more of these pastoralists are turning to a sedentary life because of the increasing difficulty of maintaining their herds in a less supportive environment as well as the widespread migration of people from rural areas to the cities.

As in many hierarchical Sahelian societies, one finds nobles or free people at the top and the descendants of captives at the bottom, with craftspeople in a less-defined position between the two.

Guro

The Guro are a Mande people who lived some distance south of the Mande heartland in the Mali-Guinea border region. They are believed to have migrated south to the central region of Côte d'Ivoire at least two centuries ago. They lived in an area marked by both forest and savanna on the banks of the Bandama River. To escape invading French forces in the early twentieth century, they left their villages and moved to the bush from 1906 to 1912.

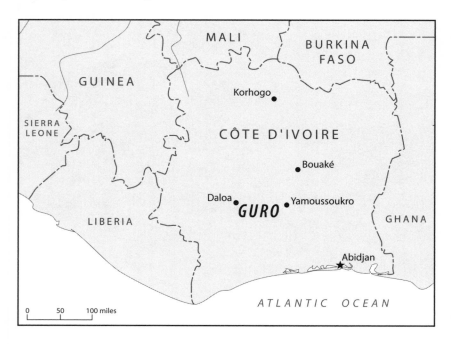

Political power was traditionally held by a council of male elders. They did not have chiefs. Until the 1980s, the Guro were farmers, hunters, weavers, and traders, but today they focus mainly on agriculture. They grow a variety of crops, including rice, yams, coffee, cotton, and cocoa. The Guro number about a half million.

They are of patrilineal descent. A young woman's marriage is a necessary precondition for her younger brother's or a patrilineal cousin's marriage. The goods given by her future husband's family to her patrilineal lineage or family are used to obtain a spouse for her brother or for her father's brother's son, or cousin. For this reason, a lineage's daughter is considered to be socially superior to a wife.

Hausa

The diverse Hausa-speaking peoples live mostly in northern Nigeria and neighboring eastern Niger, but have spread throughout West Africa, including Ghana and Cameroon. Fifty million people speak Hausa as a primary or secondary language. It is probable that more people speak Hausa than any other language in West Africa.

In the seventeenth century, as Islam began to spread more widely in West Africa, the Hausa joined with the Fulbe to create more powerful kingdoms. The

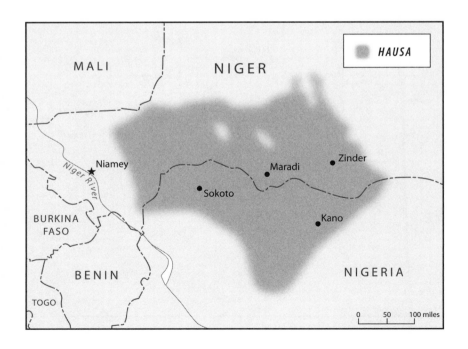

Hausa became widely known for maintaining a network of long-distance trade from West Africa across the Sahara to North Africa.

During the colonization of Nigeria, the Hausa were able to maintain much of their influence in their city-states under the system of indirect rule established by the British. One outcome was that the rulers were able to play a powerful role in the politics of Nigeria, especially after independence.

In Niger, the first capital of the colony was established in 1911 in Zinder, the major city in the eastern region where the Hausa live. Although in 1926 the French transferred the capital to Niamey in the Songhoy-Zarma area, the Hausa continued to play a significant role in commerce.

Jula

The Jula (Dyula, Dioula) are a Mande people who live mostly in the central and eastern parts of northern Côte d'Ivoire. Jula, closely related to Bamana, is spoken in Burkina Faso, Côte d'Ivoire, and Gambia. The term *jula* conveys the concept of trader, and more particularly Muslim trader. The Jula adopted Islam in order to establish closer contacts with their partners in long-distance trade.

The protection of trade was a powerful motivation for the establishment in the seventeenth century of the Gonja state, between northern Ghana and central Mali. After the decline of Gonja, and under the leadership of Seku Wattara,

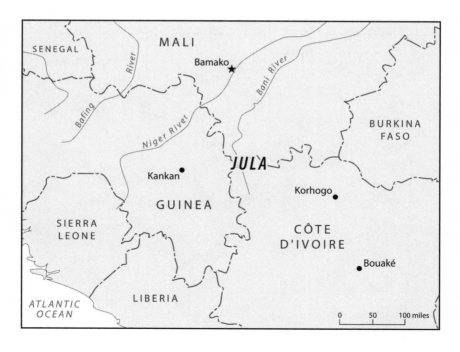

the Jula created a city-state in 1710 in what is today northern Côte d'Ivoire. This city became eventually the Kong empire, and in the nineteenth century it became very powerful both because of its role in trade between European merchants on the coast and peoples to the north, and also because of its access to rifles.

During the late nineteenth century, the most powerful resister against French conquest, Samory Touré, brought the Jula into his empire as allies. But that political relationship, which benefited the Jula's commercial tradition, ended after the capture of Samory Touré and the conquest of the entire region of Mali, Guinea, and Côte d'Ivoire by the French.

As in other societies in the Sahel and nearby regions, the Jula are patriarchal and patrilineal, with a social structure organized with free people or nobles at the top, those of captive origin at the bottom, and craftspeople occupying their own place to some extent outside the hierarchy.

Khassonké

The Khassonké live in an area called Khasso in southwestern Mali that includes the cities of Kayes, Kita, and Bafoulabé. Khassonké is part of the Mande family of languages. Originally a Malinké state, Khasso fell under Fulbe control in the late eighteenth century, and the state developed under the leadership of Demba

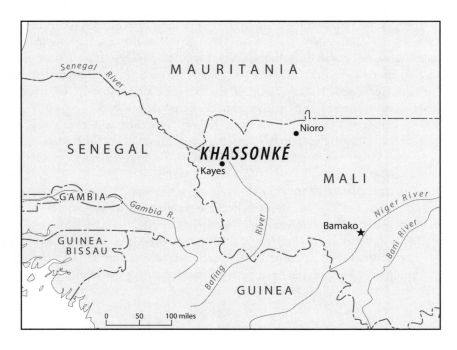

Sega. By the mid-nineteenth century, the kingdom began to disintegrate into small city-states as the result of conflicts between different factions. These principalities developed alliances with other states and kingdoms in order to survive. At some point, the French, who were developing commercial interests in the region, became involved in these changing alliances.

In 1855 El Hadj Umar conquered Khasso's city-states. One outcome was that Khasso became a buffer between El Hadj's kingdom and the French in the upper Senegal River region. A series of conflicts and alliances involving the Khassonké, the Tukolor empire of Amadou (son of Umar Tall), and other peoples in the region during the next three decades had a negative impact on the expansion of French trade inland. The French conquered most of the region by 1880, and the influence of Khasso declined considerably.

The Khassonké today are of mixed Fulbe and Malinké origin, as evidenced in clan names and other traditions. Today, the Khassonké are largely an agricultural people with traditional Islamic and patriarchal values and beliefs. Like other peoples in the Sahel, the Khassonké are migrating to cities in search of new opportunities.

Lebu

The Lebu (Lébou) live primarily on the coast of Senegal. They have deep roots in Wolof and Serer cultures. Today, they speak Wolof with a Lebu accent. They migrated to the Cap Vert region in the sixteenth century to escape domination by the Wolof. There, they established in the late eighteenth century a republic based on assemblies in cities in the Dakar region and a larger assembly representing all communities. On several occasions, the Lebu were obliged to flee to the island of Gorée, a few kilometers off the shore of Dakar, and down the coast in order to escape attacks by armies from the kingdom of Cayor.

One consequence of their presence in the region of the Cap Vert peninsula is that they had early contact with French traders. Marriages of the traders and Lebu and Serer women created an aristocracy with much influence in their communities.

With a population of 200,000, the Lebu are a very small minority of the 14 million citizens of Senegal. The Lebu have long maintained a close relationship with another minority, the Serer, who number 1.5 million.

The Lebu are primarily fishermen and farmers, though in recent years they have been increasingly active in construction and real estate in the Dakar area. Predominantly Muslim, the Lebu have maintained strong ties with their pre-Islamic system of beliefs based on ancestors and on their close relationship with the sea.

Malinké

The Malinké are a Mande people who live primarily in western Mali and northern Guinea and in parts of Senegal, Mauritania, Guinea-Bissau, Gambia, and Côte d'Ivoire. They speak Maninka. According to their oral tradition, their leader Sundiata Keita founded the empire of Mali in the thirteenth century and expanded it to cover a larger swath of the western Sahel region from Gambia to Burkina Faso. The capital was eventually at Kangaba, which is today a village in southwestern Mali near the border with Guinea. After defeating the Sosso, a people from southern Guinea, the Malinké played a dominant role in the trans-Saharan trade in the western area of the Sahel. The empire of Mali reached its apogee under the rule of Mansa Musa from 1312 to 1327; he was best known for his pilgrimage to Mecca in 1324–1325 with a large entourage and so much gold that the value of the metal declined in Cairo when he stopped there. The rise of the Songhoy empire to the east in the late fifteenth century and internal conflicts led to the decline of the Mali empire.

The Malinké are primarily sedentary agricultural people, but they also fish, trade, and raise cattle. Predominantly Muslim, Malinké society is composed of the freeborn, artisans, and those who are descended from captives. Those

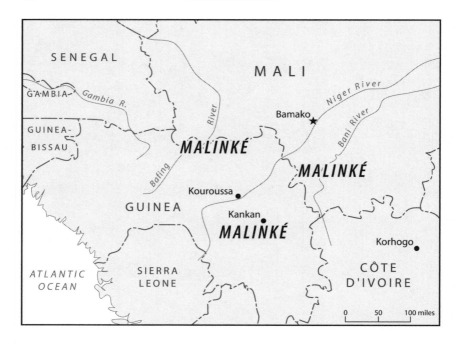

of noble or freeborn status are traders and farmers. Malinké artisans, or *nya-makala,* are known for their skills with metal, wood, cloth, and words, the specialty of the griots.

Mandinka

The Mandinka are one of the many Mande peoples who claim roots in the Mali empire. They migrated west from the Niger River basin in search of more fertile land. The Malinké converted to Islam during the nineteenth century. Numbering 500,000, they constitute the largest ethnic group in Gambia. Another half million live today in Burkina Faso, Côte d'Ivoire, Guinea, Guinea-Bissau, Liberia, Mali, Senegal, and Sierra Leone. The main language of Gambia, Mandinka is related to Bamana.

The Mandinka, along with other peoples in the region, established trade relations with the Portuguese, French, and British at different times from the fifteenth to the nineteenth centuries. During the seventeenth and eighteenth centuries, France and Britain competed for control over the Senegambian region. During the slave trade, many Mandinka and people from other groups were shipped to Europe and later to North America and the West Indies. Gambia became a British colony in 1889.

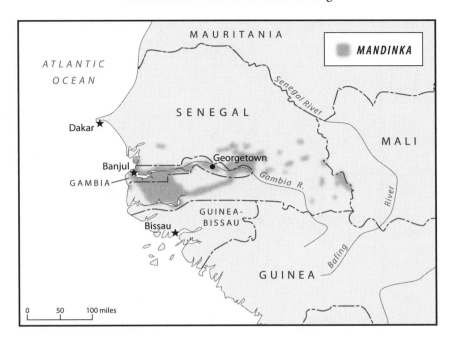

The Mandinka are agriculturalists who grow millet, rice, and peanuts. They also fish on the Gambia and Casamance rivers. Mandinka society is marked by patriarchy and hierarchy, with nobles superior to those of captive origin. Craftspeople, including weavers, woodworkers, blacksmiths, and griots, occupy a separate position that does not fit neatly into the hierarchy of nobles and former captives. The Mandinka are best known outside of their region for the vocal and instrumental music of their griots, who, as in other parts of the Sahel, maintain the history of the people.

Moors

The Moors live primarily in Mauritania, a large but sparsely populated country of 3 million people. They are also found in neighboring Morocco, Algeria, Senegal, and Mali. They speak Hassaniya, a variant of Arabic influenced by the language of the Berber or, as they prefer to be known today, the Amazigh. The Moors are a blend of people of Amazigh, Arab, and sub-Saharan origin who are distinguished from Arabs in other countries by their dialect of Arabic, which Arabophones to the east find difficult to understand, and by the diversity of their skin color, which ranges from white to black. Scholars do not agree on whether the Moors constitute a distinct ethnic group.

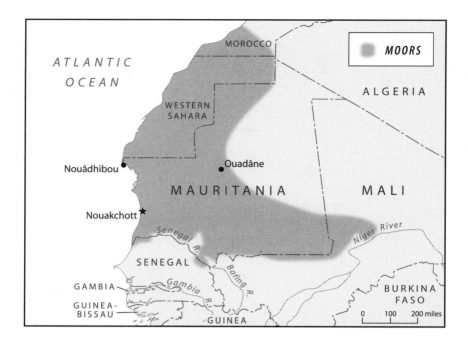

After invading Spain in the eighth century, Moors created an Islamic culture centered in southern Spain in what became known as Andalusia. They were driven back to North Africa by the Spanish at the end of the fifteenth century.

The Moors in North Africa were defeated in the eleventh century by Arab armies led by Beni Hassan. Today, the descendants of these Arab warriors make up the highest class in a hierarchy that includes sub-Saharan Africans, many of whom are descended from slaves imported for centuries by the Moors. Today, Mauritania continues to be criticized by other countries because of evidence of slavery. The number of people who live in a subservient situation that many term slavery has been estimated at 20 percent.

Moor society is patriarchal, hierarchical, and Islamic. Agriculture, animal raising, mining, and ocean fishing are mainstays of the economy of Mauritania.

Mossi

The Mossi live in Burkina Faso, formerly known as Upper Volta. Their population of 6 million constitutes 40 percent of the country. There are also large communities of Mossi in neighboring countries such as Ghana, Niger, and

Côte d'Ivoire. Their language, Moré (Mooré), is the lingua franca of Burkina Faso, and they play a dominant role in politics and commerce.

The Mossi trace their history back to a series of kingdoms founded in the eleventh, twelfth, and fifteenth centuries. The rulers resisted Fulbe armies that spread from west to east in the Sahel in the nineteenth century. All of the kingdoms survived these invasions until the arrival of the French at the end of the nineteenth century, when the notoriously violent Voulet-Chanoine expedition swept eastward through their region, encountering stiff resistance from the Azna people led by Queen Sarraounia Mangou in Niger. The only kingdom in Burkina Faso to survive the French conquest was Yatenga, whose ruler, the Moro Naba, signed a treaty with the colonizers in 1895. His descendants continue to hold a privileged position in Burkina Faso today.

Resistant to Islam until the nineteenth century, the Mossi have become much more accepting of the religion. Today, 60 percent are Muslim and 20 percent Christian, but many people have also maintained an attachment to their traditional system of belief, rooted in the worship of ancestors.

The Mossi are primarily an agricultural people who grow millet, sorghum, maize, sesame, peanuts, and indigo. Their social organization is hierarchical and patriarchal.

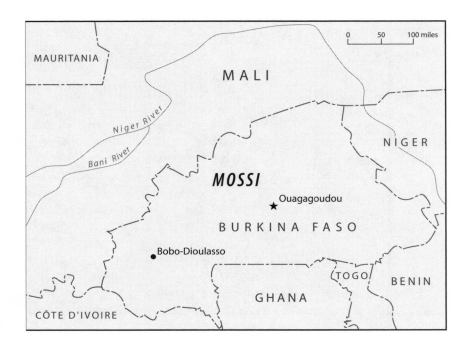

Serer

The Serer are believed to have migrated to central Senegal from the northeast in the tenth to thirteenth centuries. They established kingdoms in the Sine and Saloum regions and were vassals of the Jolof kingdom of the Wolof until the end of the nineteenth century. There is a traditional belief that the Wolof descended from the Serer. Today, the Serer are the third-largest ethnic group in Senegal with 1.5 million people living mainly in the region between Dakar and Gambia. They also constitute minority populations in Gambia and Mauritania.

Agriculturalists, they produce millet, rice, and other crops. A growing number of Serer have migrated to Dakar to seek work.

Although they long resisted the introduction of Islam into their region, they began to adopt the religion at the beginning of the nineteenth century. But as is the case with other Sahelian peoples, the Serer have not entirely abandoned their traditional system of belief. Its distinguishing characteristic is monotheism.

The Serer are notable in Senegal for their wrestlers and for their contributions to political life. The first two presidents of Senegal were Serer: Léopold Sédar Senghor from 1960 to 1980 and Abdou Diouf, 1981–2000.

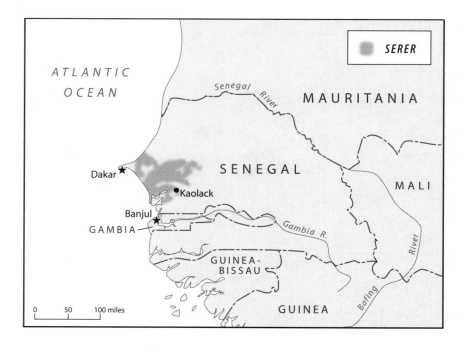

In Serer society, inheritance and succession are matrilineal. They maintain a hierarchical social structure with chiefs and freeborn people at the top, those descended from captives at the bottom, and artisans in a separate category of their own.

Songhoy

The peoples who speak Songhoy (Songhay, Songhai, Sonrai) live along the Niger River from Mali down through Niger to northern Benin and northwestern Nigeria, with small communities in Burkina Faso and Ghana. They are closely related to the Zarma. Linguists believe that the Songhoy language is the result of contacts long ago between peoples from the desert and those living along the river.

Under the leadership of Sonni Ali Ber, the Songhoy in the late fifteenth century built an enormous empire, swallowing up most of the earlier Mali empire. The capital was Gao on the Niger River in eastern Mali. Askia Mohammed brought the empire to its apogee from 1493 to 1528. He was well known for his support of clerics in Timbuktu and his pilgrimage to Mecca in 1497–1498. Many Sahelian peoples remember his efforts to spread Islam by persuasion and

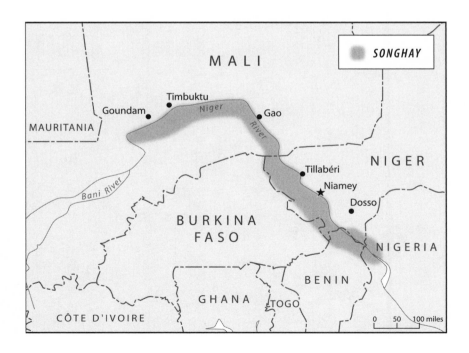

by force. The empire declined after his death in 1528, and ended in 1591 when a Moroccan army defeated the Songhoy.

Songhoy society was matrilineal before the arrival of Islam and European colonialism. Today, the Songhoy are Islamic, hierarchical, and both matrilineal and patriarchal. The society is composed of nobles, artisans, and descendants of captives, but these distinctions are breaking down as the result of greater access to Western-style education and migration to cities. The Songhoy are for the most part farmers who produce rice and millet, but those who live along the shore and on islands in the Niger River are well known for their skill at fishing.

Soninké

The Soninké, also known as the Sarakollé, were one of the earliest sub-Saharan peoples to adopt Islam as a result of their contact with Muslim traders traveling south from Morocco and Algeria in the tenth century. Around the same time, they founded the Ghana empire, known as Wagadu, in southeastern Mauritania and northwestern Mali. The decline of the empire in the eleventh century led to the dispersion of the Soninké across West Africa. Those who remained in the upper Senegal River region established the kingdom of Galam. The

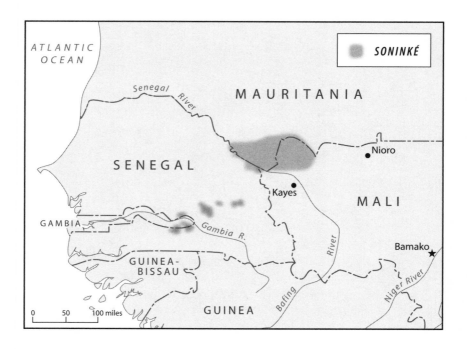

Soninké participated in riverine trade with the French in the seventeenth and eighteenth centuries. In the nineteenth century, however, they resisted French attempts to colonize Senegal.

Today, 1 million Soninké live in Mali, with smaller populations in Senegal, Mauritania, Gambia, and Côte d'Ivoire adding up to another million. Communities are also found in Guinea-Bissau, Sierra Leone, Burkina Faso, Democratic Republic of Congo, and France. Soninké laborers have the highest rate of migration in the Sahel. As with many other peoples, they have established colonies in several African countries, in Europe, and in North America. The Soninké language is a northern branch of the large Mande family of languages.

The Soninké are known as farmers and traders. Today, they are also active in real estate in Dakar, Bamako, elsewhere in Africa, and other parts of the world.

Their society is hierarchical and patrilineal. However, with the emigration of so many young males, leaving women, old men, and children behind, a form of what has been called matriarchy has developed.

Tuareg

The Tuareg (Touareg) call themselves Imazighen or Kel Tamashek. There are 6 million Tuareg in Niger, Mali, Algeria, Libya, and Burkina Faso. Pastoral nomads, they also played a central role in trans-Saharan trade until the twentieth century. Today, as the result of drought and other conditions, they are becoming semi-nomadic or sedentary, living in villages, towns, and cities. Tuareg speak Tamashek, a southern Berber language, and they maintain a very old system of writing called Tifinar, believed to be rooted in a pre-Roman script of the Numidians in North Africa.

Organized into confederations, the Tuareg warred often with the sedentary peoples to the south. When Sahelian countries obtained independence in 1960, the Tuareg became marginalized. When Niger and Mali underwent difficult transitions to democracy, some of the Tuareg launched rebellions. Today, some Tuareg continue to resist any control over their freedom to move throughout the Sahara.

The Tuareg are mostly Muslims, but many have never abandoned their pre-Islamic beliefs and practices. Their stratified society includes nobles, vassals, artisans, and those who live with them in a subservient relationship often described as slavery. These people manage herds and perform other manual tasks. Today, social distinctions are beginning to blur as more Tuareg and their vassals migrate to cities in search of work.

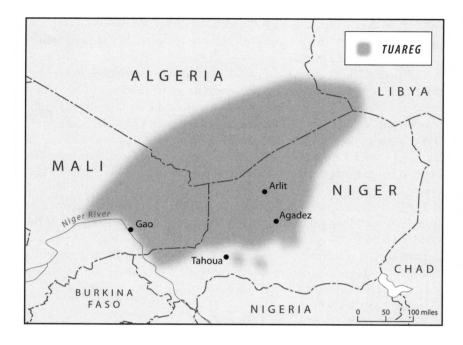

The men are noted for their tradition of wearing a blue veil, and the women for the high degree of social freedom they enjoy as well as the fact that they do not wear veils.

Wolof

The Wolof live in the region from southern Mauritania, on the right bank of the Senegal River, to the Gambia River in the south. The Wolof kingdom, called Jolof, dates from the fourteenth century and eventually included the vassal states of Cayor, Waalo, Baol, Sine, and Saloum. At the end of the sixteenth century, these states broke away from Jolof. Jolof and its former vassal states were destroyed in the late nineteenth century during the French conquest of Senegal.

Predominantly Muslims, the Wolof are the source of Islamic brotherhoods such as the Mourides. They are a powerful cultural, religious, and economic influence in Senegal. Today, although the Wolof comprise less than half of the 12 million people of Senegal, most Senegalese speak the language, and the Wolof play a role in society that is disproportionate to their numbers.

Wolof society was originally matrilineal, but today it is patrilineal in part because of Islamic and French influence. It is a hierarchical system composed of nobles or freeborn, artisans, and those of captive origin. This structure is

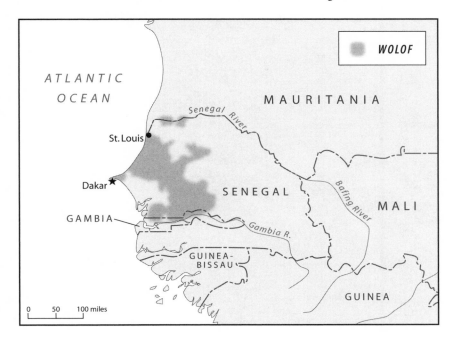

weakening, however, as a result of Western influence and migration from villages to cities.

The Wolof are largely an agricultural people who have depended on the production of millet and peanuts. Some of them are also herders and fishermen. But as the price of agricultural products declines and the conditions for raising animals become more difficult, more Wolof are emigrating to countries in Africa, Europe, and North America, especially France and the United States, in search of work.

Zarma

The Zarma (Zerma, Djerma) live on the left bank of the Niger River, from the Mali border south to northern Benin. The Zarma language is very close to Songhoy, and the two peoples are often linked under the term Songhoy-Zarma. According to their oral history, they migrated from Mali many centuries ago, perhaps from Malinké or Soninké areas. According to this account, they were led by a legendary leader named Mali Bero. They settled in western Niger in Ouallam, Filingué, Dosso, the Boboye, and the region around Niamey. But they came under continual pressure from the Tuareg to the north and the Fulbe to the west and south.

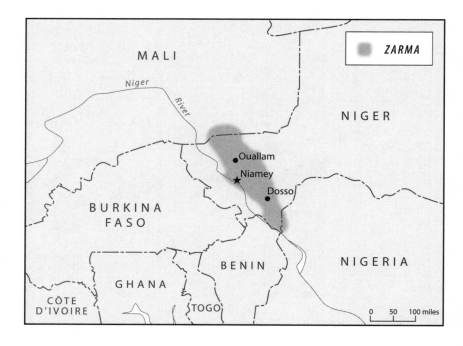

Their city-states were Islamic, matriarchal, and hierarchical. Each was led by a *zarmakoy* (*zermakoye*), sometimes chosen in rotating fashion from the leading families. The *zarmakoy* of Dosso became one of the most powerful of these leaders. In 1898, when a French column arrived in Dosso from the coast, Zarmakoy Aouta negotiated a treaty with the invaders that fixed power in his family and enabled his descendants to play a major role in the politics of Niger for many generations.

The Zarma farm the dry riverbed areas of western Niger and the fertile regions of the Boboye. They have to work hard to produce millet, sorghum, and maize from land that is only marginally suited for agriculture. For this reason, many Zarma men migrate to the cities and to the coast to find work during the long dry season from October to May.

SONG SUBJECTS AND GENRES

There are many ways to organize song lyrics. We have chosen to begin with the large corpus of songs about marriage, one of the most important events in the life of a woman and also the source of many of her concerns. Songs about fertility, birth, and the care of children follow. Then, we present a collection that reveals the surprisingly diverse roles of women in society. The last chapter includes songs about women's attitudes toward death.

We recognize that any attempt to categorize forms or subjects of verbal art is at best limited because women often mix different themes in the same performance. Furthermore, the occasions for these songs may differ, depending on the practices of each people. Nevertheless, in the juxtaposition of lyrics on similar topics or sung for similar events, for example those sung at the arrival of a second wife in the compound of the husband, it quickly becomes apparent that in many cases the specificity of each society is matched by similarities in the concerns of women from Senegal eastward.

The songs collected here are part of particular genres. For example, for the Songhoy of Niger, the *zamu* is a praise song for children that may focus on a variety of subjects, but especially beauty. The name of the genre echoes those of similar forms throughout the Sahel that often include a wider range of praises—for example, *jamu* among the Mande and *jammude* for the Fulbe. The Lebu and Wolof *taasu* genre includes songs that both praise and mock their subjects. The Wolof *xaxar* and the Songhoy *marchande,* though not entirely similar, include songs designed to criticize a new wife who joins a family where there are already one or more wives. Some of the genres convey information about a broad topic—for example, what appears to be a form of hierarchy governing relations between two different types of women. But in each local context, the reasons for the distinctions between the women are quite different. For example, in the *kanyalen* songs of the Casamance region of Senegal recorded by Kirsten Langeveld, the unfortunate woman who has lost children is transferred by ritual into a lower social category. By contrast, the *maani fori* songs recorded by Sidikou in Niger mark a distinction between women of different sizes: the fat women treat their thin sisters as inferior members of society. Both genres indicate a need for more research on the notion of hierarchy among women in the region.

FORMAT OF THE ANTHOLOGY

There are over 80 songs in this collection from more than 40 researchers. The length of the songs varies from one or two verses that are repeated numerous times to as many as 190. They were collected from 1915 to 2009. In some cases, the researcher has indicated the date and place of the recording, but for many others, this information is not available. Most of the songs are from singers who normally perform in their local context, a village or a town, and are not well known outside of this area. But some of the singers have performed throughout a region or have reached wider audiences by radio broadcasts. A few songs are by well-known singers who have appeared publicly in Africa or in Europe.

One result of the diversity of the sources is that the reader will find considerable variation in the presentation of the lyrics. Some will have numbered lines, following the format chosen by the researcher, while others will have no numbers. Although it is often the custom to insert an *x* plus a number (e.g., x8) at the end of a line to indicate repetition, we usually include all repetitions of lines because the singing of a verse many times often has particular meaning in the context of an event. In most song examples, we have included all the lyrics that were collected, but we have chosen occasionally to include excerpts from a much longer song or an incomplete version published by a researcher because of the way the lyrics illustrate one of the categories.

We will introduce each song and then include any necessary explanations of terms—those of the researcher or our own. Occasionally, translations or explanations of terms will appear within the song. Songs will be presented in the English translation provided by the researcher who made the original recording. Where the lyrics as originally recorded were translated by the researcher into French, we have translated them into English, though we recognize that this second step away from the original African language compounds the problem of conveying meaning accurately. For a selection of songs, we have included the original transcription in an appendix.

For those interested in learning more about a particular song or genre, papers from the meeting in Princeton in 2003 and other contributions will be included in a forthcoming companion volume titled *New Perspectives in Research on Women's Songs from the Sahel*. For songs chosen from other sources, the reader can find the name of the collector and the title of the source in the bibliography.

Song Lyrics

1 —ᕝ *Marriage*

Any collection of songs about marriage, an event of enormous importance for a woman and her family, must include many facets, including love, courtship, women's attitudes toward this institution, and the choice of a husband—by the family or by the bride. The wedding can be an affair that lasts several days and includes a variety of events: the departure of the bride from her house, her reception in her husband's home, and the giving of advice on how to prepare for sexual activity, how to relate with in-laws, and how to respond to abuse.

ATTITUDES TOWARD MARRIAGE

A woman contemplating marriage may be concerned about the nature of the relationship with the man she might marry, or even the entire concept of marriage. In the following Wolof wedding song, recorded in Senegal from Wolof griottes by Marame Gueye (2003), the woman expresses ambivalence about marriage. But in the end, she reveals that she has decided to get married. The reference to the mortar and pestle is not simply to two basic tools for husking grain but is charged with sexual connotations.

> I am not getting married yet
> I am not getting married yet mother
> Your little girl is still young.
> The mortar and the pestle are here
> Mother let me whisper something to you
> Your little girl is still young.
> Today's men no longer respect their wives
> When they make claims they abuse them
> Marriage should not mean bondage.
> I have been waiting for too long.
> I am going to get married now
> I am going to get married now mother

Today's women are no longer good wives
I could before and now I can't
Is not what a married woman should say.

ARRANGED MARRIAGES

One reason for concern on the part of future brides is the possibility of an arranged marriage, a practice that is becoming less and less common as young women assert the right to choose their own husband. But some marriages still are arranged in order to maintain or create new family ties for economic, social, or political reasons. In the Bamana song below, collected by Luneau in 1967–1968 in the village of Beleko, Mali (1981:50–51; 2010:43), a woman's refusal to accept an arranged marriage is marked by an intensity that matches that of the Zarma song that follows it.

My father and my mother, I've said it to you
I am going to kill myself
I am going to kill myself
My father and my mother, I've said it to you
Who have given me in marriage
Don't sell me

Don't sell me like a slave
I've said it to you.
Don't sell me like a slave
My father and my mother, I've said it to you,
I am going to kill myself.

In the following Zarma song, recorded by Aissata Niandou in Niger (2003), the woman asks her mother to kill her if she has to marry a man with another wife.

If I were to marry a married man
Let my mother push me
In some boiling porridge,
Let my mother push me
In some boiling porridge.
Before the porridge gets done,
I'll be well cooked too.

A striking example of how a woman manages to avoid an arranged marriage in order to wed her lover appears in a well-known song titled "Sara." It was sung by Siramori Diabaté in 1968 and recorded by Charles Bird (1997:114–123).

In the song, Sara has given her word that she will marry a man whom she does not love. In order to stop the well-advanced preparations for the wedding, she feigns illness—pain in her stomach. No one seems able to cure her. She finally turns to her lover, "her secret-sharer," who, as described in this brief excerpt, finds the cure and therefore earns the right to marry her.

"Ah! Baba!" she said: "My belly has cooled,
Baba, ah, my belly has cooled, lalala! Woyi!
My belly has cooled today.
I passed the night my belly did not rise up.
Baba, my belly has cooled.
Make this my true wedded husband."
Sara's mother said: "Won't you calm down!
The late afternoon prayer has not been called.
And you say your belly has been cooled!"
"Mama, won't you prepare the baggage today?
Prepare my wedding baggage today.
Let my wedding-arrangers come forward.
This one will be my true wedded husband."

MAY-DECEMBER MARRIAGES

Some marriages are between a man and woman of similar age, but others involve a much older man. He may persuade members of the bride's family of the benefits of marriage between the daughter and him for some of the reasons cited above. It is not surprising that opposition to these arrangements usually comes from younger women, while the older women see the benefits. Often, aunts or other female relatives serve as intermediaries in promoting May–December marriages. Ousmane Sembène offers a striking example in his film *Xala* (1973) when a much older man takes a high school student as his third wife thanks in large part to the connivance of the girl's aunt, who counts on benefits for the entire family from the marriage.

In the song below, the singer describes both the advantages of accepting an older man as a husband and the problems that can occur with a younger spouse. Luneau explains in a note that the problem with a young man is that if he makes a mistake he can bring a curse down upon himself from his parents, and the bride will suffer as a result (1974:615–616; 2010:44). This, by implication, is unlikely to happen with an older husband.

The wife of an old man
If you become the wife of an old man
You will be fat and happy

While the wife of a young man
Is dull and meager
Is dull and meager

In the sack of an old man
There are fish
In the sack of an old man
There is meat

In the pocket of the old man
There is money
In the pocket of the old man
There is money

The wife of an old man
If you become the wife of an old man
You will be fat and satisfied
While the wife of a young man
Is dull and meager

In the home of a young man
There is a whip
In the home of a young man
There is a whip

In the pocket of the young man
There is a curse
In the pocket of the young man
There is a curse

The wife of an old man
If you become the wife of an old man
You will be fat and satisfied
While the wife of a young man
Is dull and meager

In the home of the young man
There is a rope
In the home of the young man
There is a rope to tie you down.

Wife of a young man
If you become the wife of a young man
You will wilt.

The woman who marries a young man
Is dull and meager

The wife of an old man
If you become the wife of an old man
You will be fat and satisfied
While the wife of a young man
Is dull and meager.

COURTSHIP

If a woman is able to avoid an arranged marriage and choose her own mate, the process begins with courtship that, from her point of view, must produce a degree of trust developing slowly over time. If the courtship proceeds too rapidly as a result of a sudden interest, it could lead to early sex and abandonment, as described in the first song below.

When the relationship progresses, the path toward marriage involves not only the two partners, but also entire families and clans. Members of each family must agree that the partner chosen by their child is appropriate. Emissaries, often griots or griottes, must be sent to report on the history of each family. Part of the courtship process may involve the frequent distribution of small gifts to members of the bride's family.

The lyrics for these songs are remarkably similar across the Sahel. In the song below, recorded by Luneau (1981:153; 2010:121), the singer warns that she will not succumb to just any man who comes to court her. The *balafon,* to which the voice of the suitors is compared, is a type of xylophone.

The men of today
The men of today
The men of today
When they go in search of a woman
Speak in a voice that is sweeter than that of a balafon
May no one come to cajole me
To then, between home and bush,
Reject me.

LOVE

There are many different ways of expressing love, and different genres for doing so. For example, *zamu* poems among the Songhoy and Zarma consist of praising generic names and, by extension, the individuals who bear them. These songs may include expressions of love. In the song below, published by Bisilliat and Laya, a woman has fallen in love with a man well known for his ability to produce a large harvest. His success comes from the proximity of his fields to the village, a rich source of manure. But the singer cannot reach him now because he is in another village. Worse, bad times have hit her family and her nice clothing is now in tatters. Finally, the man's family does not want her to become involved with their son.

Bisilliat and Laya explain (1972:141) that the *kuubu* catching her hair is a prickly bush, *Hu-Hinza* is the place to which the loved one has gone, *talhana* is a plant that blossoms year-round, and *nime* is a widely planted, drought-resistant, and fast-growing tree that provides many benefits. The term *vomit* below refers to rejection.

Maadugu who has beautiful ears of millet at the edge of the village.
I love Maadugu
I don't like the mother of Maadugu
The wicked mother of Maadugu
She is the one who told him to send me away

The man who has beautiful ears of millet at the edge of the village
Envelop him in incense, put incense on him, and have him sit down
The man who has beautiful ears of late millet at the edge of the village
I love Maadugu
I will not vomit Maadugu
The wicked mother of Maadugu
She is the one who told him to send me away

I was walking and while walking, I was turning back
Until I arrived home
Until a thorn of *kuubu*
Caught my hair
I said: "branch of *kuubu*
Let go of my hair"
At the same time the light-skinned man was down there, at Hu-Hinza
The handsome light-skinned man, he is still at Hu-Hinza

The father of Maranga knows how to attract misfortune
What we were last year, we are not this year
Last year at this time I was a sweet potato
Last year at this time I was a *talhana*
Last year at this time I was a *nime*
Last year I wore an embroidered wrapper
This year, I have only rags to tie around my waist.

In the following brief song recorded by Niandou (2003), which could also have been placed with those about arranged marriages, the narrator declares quite openly her love for one man and warns the elders not to interfere.

Bibata, sister of Saadu
Said "No one but Komi"
When the hearts of two young persons
Love each other
Let elders not interfere.

Finally, in the excerpt below from the song by the Hausa popular performer Zabiya Uwani Zakirai, the singer describes the physical and emotional impact of separation from her lover. The song was recorded in or before 1976 by Mohammed Sani Ibrahim, a student at Bayero University in northern Nigeria, and translated by Graham Furniss and Soulaiman Ibrahima Katsina (Furniss 1996:146–147).

I remember the day of our farewell
On the open space where we used to play,
Habibu, the schoolboy
The moon was clear and bright,
Ten days old.
Habibu and I said farewell to each other,
And for seven days I have not been able to sleep,
I have been thinking of love,
Habibu the schoolboy.
They gave me one kind of food and I said no,
They gave me another kind of food and I said no,
They gave me water and I said no.
Look how thin I have become,
All skin and bone and all dried up,
Thinking of love,
Habibu, the schoolboy.

VIRGINITY

Whatever the nature of the marriage, arranged or not, in most Sahelian cultures virginity is important, if not the sine qua non, for a "respectable" woman to marry. One can find descriptions going back several centuries of griots and griottes parading through a village with a blood-stained sheet as evidence of the bride's virginity on the morning after the wedding. For example, in 1685 the French administrator Michel Jajolet de La Courbe described how in northern Senegal the groom carried the blood-stained sheet through the village on the tip of a spear, followed by griots singing the praises of the bride (1913:31; cited in Hale 1998:87). In cases where the bride is not a virgin, women in the family sometimes make use of a convenient remedy: the blood of a chicken is sprinkled on the sheets the morning after the wedding. In the novel and film *Xala,* Ousmane Sembène includes a scene of a family member carrying a chicken for this purpose after the wedding night of the protagonist and his young third wife.

Clearly, the family of the bride-to-be is concerned about the reputation of their child. In the Wolof song below, recorded from griottes in Dakar, Senegal, by Marame Gueye (2003), the family emphasizes the value of their daughter by differentiating between women who engage in sex with men before marriage and those whose hymens are intact on the wedding night. But the message is aimed not only at those outside the woman's family—in particular, the family of the groom—but, more important, at the future bride herself and all young women. Virginity is of great value both for them and for their families. The necklace in the song symbolizes the tradition of virginity that goes back several generations among the women of the family, and CFA franc (Communauté Financière Africaine) is the local currency.

The necklace, where is the necklace?
The necklace that your grandmother wore and handed over to your mother
You will wear today.
Men are not stupid.
Men's mothers are not stupid.
If a girl is serious, they will marry her
If a girl is not serious, they will fuck her and leave her to be a burden to her
    mother.
My daughter was born with underwear
She took it off last night.
Tell me where you bred her so that she could escape men
For me to breed my daughters there.
Whoever has a daughter should bring her to you.
The chicken has sent me
And I must tell it all.
It says that it is not afraid and none of her relatives is afraid,
It is not dead and none of her relatives is dead.
There is a vagina among vaginas,
One buys it with fifty thousand CFA [US$100]
A watch and a boombox,

A television set and a jewelry box.
But there is a vagina among vaginas,
One buys it with only a bottle of beer.
I prefer a silent vagina to a vagina that honks like a car
Vagina, vagina, vagina, vagina!
Its name is not vagina
Its real name is treasure.
Whoever spoils it does not know it
A nice house!
From the vagina!
A nice car!
From the vagina!
A box of jewels!
From the vagina!
A television set!
From the vagina!
Honoring your mother!
From the vagina!
Honoring your paternal aunts!
From the vagina!
Honoring your friends!
From the vagina!
Honoring oneself!
From the vagina!
The hymen is very small.
If you want to feed yourself and your mother [from] it,
There will be nothing left of it.

ADVICE TO THE BRIDE

As the bride approaches the time for the wedding, the women around her—her mother, aunts, and other relatives involved in the preparations for the event—offer a variety of advice on how to deal with the challenges of moving into the home of her in-laws after the wedding. Songs containing advice are among the most common across the Sahel. But the advice is not limited to the bride, as the song directed at the groom and his family illustrates.

The excerpts below are from the traditional song "Worotan" by Oumou Sangare, a professional singer from the Ouassoulou region of southern Mali. It was released by her British label, World Circuit, in 1996. *Worotan* is a Bamana term referring to the "ten kola nuts" that, as Durán explains (1999:19), are given by the groom's family to the bride's family as a symbol that seals the agreement for the marriage.

> Young brides, be careful when you first go to your husband's house
> for everywhere there are traps laid to test you
> dear young wives, once you are living with your husband's family
> do not touch the money that you see under the mattress when you
> are doing housework
> it's there to test you . . .
> marriage is a test of endurance because
> the price of a mere ten kola nuts turns the bride into a slave.

In another Wolof song, also collected by Gueye (2003), the singer from the family of the bride warns the groom about what will happen if he is abusive toward his new wife.

> Don't hit her, don't insult by the mother
> Be patient with her
> If you hit her or insult her by the mother
> She will soon leave
> Don't hit her, don't insult the mother
> Be patient with her
> [If] you hit her or insult by the mother
> We will soon take her back.

Two versions of the same song advising the bride to leave the home of her husband suggest that the roots of this topic are very deep and have changed little over time. The first was collected in 1958 and published by Sidikou over four decades later. The other was recorded by Hale three decades after the first was collected, and the performance appears in the video *Griottes of the Sahel: Female Keepers of the Songhay Oral Tradition in Niger* (1990).

> If your mother-in-law scolds you,
> Cry and hush
> If your father-in-law insults you,
> Cry and hush
> If your elder brother-in-law insults you,
> Cry and hush
> If your younger sister and brothers-in-law insult you
> Cry and hush.
> If your husband himself insults your mother,
> Take your belongings,

Because doing that is not a shame,
For a newlywed. (Sidikou 2001:37)

The following song, "Stop Crying Bride" by Weybi Karma, recorded by Hale in 1989 in Niamey, Niger (1990, 1998), echoes the same warning. The repetition of two lines near the end of the song about abuse from the bride's mother-in-law underscores the importance of the solution offered in the final lines.

Stop crying, stop crying bride,
Stop crying and listen to me.
If your in-laws abuse you,
Just cry but don't say anything.
If your sisters-in-law abuse you,
Just cry but don't say anything.
If your husband's mother abuses you,
Just cry but don't say anything.
If your husband's mother abuses you,
Just cry but don't say anything.
But leaving your home
Is not a crime.

THE WEDDING

The Departure of the Bride

The departure of the bride from her family's house prior to the wedding ceremony marks the first step on the road to her integration into the family of the groom. It represents both the difficult good-bye to her own family and the start of what may be a challenging new situation.

In the following excerpt from "Worotan," parts of which were also cited earlier, the listener hears two points of view on the departure, that of the bride and that of her mother. The song also offers a before-and-after perspective, with the first part taking place at the home of the bride, and the second part at the home of the groom. The italicized lines in brackets are by Durán.

[*The bride's voice*]:
Ah, it's so far away [*i.e., the husband's house*].
My mother, my father,
God knows, the woman is a slave
because I am going to my husband's house. . . .
The people who are sitting here, the wedding guests
By God, they have betrayed me

because I am going to my husband's house. . . .
[*The bride's mother's voice*]:
If you go to your husband's house
If the man you marry is as old as your own father
Treat him with the same respect as your own father
Because you are a slave. . . .
[*The bride's voice; she is now in her husband's house*]:
If I speak, they [*the husband's family*] say I talk too much
if I'm silent, they say I'm too proud
if I laugh, they say I'm impolite
because I'm a slave.
When I think of it, I tremble
God knows, a woman is a slave.

The Day of the Wedding

The wedding day is full of excitement and expectation, as seen in this Jula song recorded by Diagana (1990:99). Here, the bride addresses her fiancé, Magassa, about the wedding and what they will do after they are married.

The day of our wedding has come
Magassa
The day of our wedding has come,
The wedding of the girls
Magassa
The day of the wedding
The wedding of the nubile girls
Magassa
The day of the wedding of the uncircumsized
Magassa
Here is the day of the wedding of the young adolescents.
Magassa
Here is the day of our wedding
Magassa
Are we going to climb? Climb the hills?
Magassa
Are we going to bring down[?]
Bring down the suitcases[?]
Magassa
Here is the day of our wedding.
Here is the day of our wedding.

During the festivities surrounding the wedding, many griots and griottes come to sing songs of celebration and also to seek rewards from the many relatives of the bride who are present. The Zarma song by Weybi Karma below, recorded by Hale in 1989 (1990, 1998) and translated by Aissata Niandou, is typical.

> Ask her if she knows such a day
> Ask the relatives on the mother's side if they have ever seen such a day
> Ask the relatives on the father's side if they have ever seen such a day
> Ask the younger and older sisters and brothers if they have seen such a day.
> If you see the bride's mother sitting and covering her head
> This means she has no money.
> If you see the bride's mother hiding from people
> This means she has no money in her house.
> If you see her with a long cloth, this means she has no money in the house.
> Haziya is the woman responsible for this marriage, even though she is
>   ignoring us.
> Bride, where are your older sisters and brothers?
> Where are all those older sisters and brothers?
> Where are all those younger sisters and brothers?
> Where are your father's brothers?
> Bride, where are all those grandparents you have?
> Bride, where are your older sisters and brothers?
> Where are older and younger sisters and brothers?
> I am teasing the bride but bride where are your fathers?
> Where are all those fathers you have?
> Where are your brothers, where are your brothers and sisters?

MARRIED LIFE

Polygyny

Polygyny is a custom with deep roots, both in traditional beliefs and in Islam, but it is less common today than one might believe, both for economic reasons and because younger women are less willing to accept an arrangement with more than one wife. Nevertheless, some women, especially in the rural context, freely accept the arrival of a new wife as a person who can lighten the heavy workload of maintaining a household. But even for women who accept the notion of polygyny, the arrival of a second wife, perhaps later in life when the first wife has aged, can generate a highly negative reaction, and there is a particular genre of songs aimed at second, third, and fourth wives. Given the importance of polygyny in the song tradition across the Sahel and the ubiquity of the genre, we have included several of these songs from different peoples.

The first is a lengthy Hausa song performed by the popular singer Barmani Choge. It was recorded by two undergraduate students at Bayero University in Nigeria, Musa Barah Mashi and Shekaru Umar Kaikafi, and translated by Graham Furniss and Soulaiman Ibrahima Katsina (1996:143–145). The song conveys not only the disappointment of the wife, but also her plot to destroy the marriage. In the song, *malam* is a term of respect for the woman's husband. But a *malam* is, in a more specific sense, a Muslim cleric. In many parts of the Sahel, a *malam* is believed to have special powers akin to those of sorcerers and diviners. The refrain "Allah is the light of darkness," marked by indentation, underscores the strength of the singer's adherence to Islam as she plans her break from a man whom she addresses with the respectful term *malam.* The *ablution kettle* is a simple teapot used as a container for water with which a Muslim washes his or her feet before entering a mosque and praying.

My sisters, women, relations of Fatima
Who wants to have a co-wife?
   Allah is the light of darkness
Wait a little, *sankira,* I will tell you.
I was living happily with *malam,*
Without rancor or falling out.
When I was a very young girl
I asked him to take a second wife,
And he said, "You are enough for me!"
But when he saw old age approaching,
Bearing down upon me fast,
That's when he said he wanted a second wife.
I had never so much as insulted him,
But on that day I said, "Look at this hypocrite!"
   Allah is the light in the darkness.
Whoever causes a second wife to be brought into your house,
Don't even greet them for a full nine months!
May God deal with them in his own way, day and night.
   Allah is the light in the darkness.
Wait and hear the names of a co-wife,
Black scorpion with the terrible sting!
Black snake with the terrible bite!
The bitch, the leech with a hundred mouths,

And what biting teeth, the bastard!
With teeth embedded she shakes her head to and fro.
   Allah is the light of darkness.
   Allah is the light of darkness.
I was living with my husband
A really pleasant existence,
An enjoyable life with no quarreling
   Allah is the light in the darkness.
One day my husband said to me
He wanted to take a second wife.
I said, "*Malam,* that's all right,
I will have someone to live alongside me."
   Allah is the light in the darkness.
He did not know I had my own plans,
If I am the one in charge of this house
There is no way I will allow some bitch
To come in as my co-wife.
   Allah is the light in the darkness.
As night fell,
I told my husband, "I am going out somewhere."
And I went straight to a *malam*
Who welcomed me.
   Allah is the light in the darkness.
I said, "*Malam,* I want your help,
My husband is bringing a second wife."
   Allah is the light in the darkness.
The *malam* said, "I already knew,
And I want to tell you that
This marriage will definitely go ahead,
Nothing can stop it,
But there is one small thing I can do
To help you if you want.
After this marriage has taken place
You can destroy it."
   Allah is the light in the darkness.
The *malam* gave me a potion
And said to me,
"Sprinkle this potion
Into his religious ablution kettle!"

The arrival of a co-wife can also elicit highly negative responses in song from friends of the first wife. The lyrics of these songs are in many ways formulaic. The highly insulting Wolof song below, recorded by Gueye (2003), is typical of the genre, known in Wolof as *xaxar*. Gorée is an island a little over a mile offshore from Dakar, and *axuxaa xuux* is an expression in Wolof used to make fun of men who suffer from elephantiasis or inflamed testicles.

> The "First Wives" ask:
> Doesn't the bride have friends?
> Look at the bitchy old ladies she came with.
> Doesn't the bride have friends?
> She has only one bundle and her ass.
> Looks like a seasonal worker to me!
> The "New Wives" reply:
> You don't have perfume
> You don't have incense
> You are smelly ladies!
> You don't have perfume
> You don't have incense
> Your vaginas are tiny!
> The "First Wives" respond:
> If your father claims that he went to Mecca
> He is lying
> He never got to Gorée island!
> The "New Wives" hurl back:
> You don't have soap
> You use the foam from your pussy to wash your clothes!
> *Axuxaa xuux*
> Your pussies have herpes!

From much farther east, Sidikou recorded an equally scatological song aimed at comforting the wife who will receive a co-wife and, in this case, insulting the husband who has made the decision to add a new woman to the household (2001:195–196). The song is part of a genre and a mock ceremony both called *marchande,* which is "organized by a first wife with the help of family and friends in order to ridicule her husband and her now co-wife" (46). Sidikou points out that the *marchande* is similar in some ways to the Wolof *xaxar*. Friends gather at the home of the first wife to "heal the psychological pain and wounds" resulting from the decision of her husband to take another wife. She adds that the ceremony includes dancing, often with sexual gestures and connotations.

Tobey in the fourth stanza is the rabbit, which conveys the notion of cunning and appears often in songs from the Songhoy-Zarma region. The repeated line "I was sitting down" in the last stanza means "I was already born" (195). The leaves of the *kokorbe* tree are often dried up and shriveled on the edges. The metaphor of the *kokorbe* is but one of many ways to criticize the new wife. "The heaviness of the calabashes below" refers to the strength of the first wife. She is "below" because she came first, and that position actually is positive here. "The ones on top" refers to the new wife, who is just starting her life in the new house.

1. Fulle has arrived
Fulle has arrived
May our Lord mark Fulle
Fulle is the leaf of the *kokorbe* tree
She is a *kokorbe* leaf
Beaten by the wind.

2. Mother of the house, sit well
Marriage is not a problem
Chatting is not fighting
Here comes your rival
Your luck brought her here
It is your good fate that brought her here
Hold his penis
And insert it yourself.

3. The first one is unmovable
May our Lord give the strength to the owner
Let that which hangs hang
Let the one that comes go back
If a calabash hangs it is worthless,
If a ladle hangs it is worthless
The heaviness of the calabashes below has crushed the ones on top.

4. *Tobey tobey,*
Spray pepper in our eyes
By Allah we will spray it back
Tobey tobey,
We will rub it on his testicles
So he puts it in his new wife's eyes
So he puts it in his new wife's vagina
She will not be able to sleep
She will not be able to sit.

5. Amadou Belinde
With just one testicle
The motherfucker does not even have a penis
And yet he wants to be married
I was sitting down,
When Mamoudou was circumsized
I was sitting down,
When Mamoudou was put into marriage
The one with one testicle
Is asking to be married
The one with one testicle
Does not ask to be married.

A song collected by Ariane Deluz from the Guro in Côte d'Ivoire offers a similar if less scatological scenario. The women during this recording session sang a variety of marriage-related songs before turning to what she explains as "songs of traditional insults that portray the aggressivity of co-wives" (2001:70). To the first wife, the narrator, Salimata, declares:

Binta N'Doye, the first wife of El Hadj Gueye, is favored
She knows the mind of her husband
She is already at home on the path to his field
She is close to the same age as her husband
She will understand him better than the new arrival.

A chorus responds with the insults of the first wife to the second:

Women, come to the aid of your friend
El Hadj Gueye says that he does not want a nasty woman
Awa Dione, you say that you are not leprous
But your feet are cut off, your eyes are red
And you have no nose.

The second wife replies:

I am beautiful and more cunning than the first wife of El Hadj Gueye
We will always be different
I will never be like her.

New singer:

Father of Papa Diagne, father of Abou Diagne
Root of my life
You can make me sing until I die
I love you so much that I don't dare look at you.

These negative songs are in some ways ritualized and do not necessarily foreshadow the way a new wife will be treated. But once the bride is established in the household of her husband, a variety of events or experiences may conspire to make her life there unhappy. For this reason, a bride who is accepted and appreciated by her husband's family considers herself to be fortunate. The following Songhoy-Zarma song, translated by Diouldé Laya and Fatima Moun-kaïla (2003), offers a portrait of this ideal.

> Crowned with love, and with love crowned
> Is the young woman stuffed with this stew
> Fortunate is the young woman stuffed with millet and milk
> Whoever is loved by the mother of her husband
> Is happy
> Whoever is loved by her father-in-law
> Is happy
> Whoever is loved by the siblings, brothers
> Is happy
> Happy is the one who, to the possessions of her parents,
> Sees added the kindness of the husband
> Crowned with love and with love crowned
> My daughter is happy.

Sources of Unhappiness

The fortunate situation of the daughter in the last song contrasts with those of other brides who may not find such a welcoming experience, especially in households where they are not the first wife. Although a man who has more than one wife does not necessarily preside over a family in which there is always competition and bad relations between the wives, most of the songs of complaint by brides seem to stem from these situations. The new bride may be viewed as the preferred wife by the husband, but as the lowest-ranked one by his first wife and any other wives. In order to make sure that she understands her inferior position, they may ask her to do a large share of the household work and then criticize her for not doing it well. A major source of unhappiness may be the mother-in-law or sisters-in-law, especially in the common situation where the son lives in a compound with his parents.

The following song, recorded by Niandou (2003), reflects the extent of the bride's hatred of her mother-in-law. The *gao* is a large tree that is known by different names in other parts of the Sahel. An explanation by the translators is in brackets.

> Hunchback
> Hunchback

Old woman !
If only the old woman could die!
Peace would descend [on the house]
If the old woman could lie down
Under a *gao* tree
If a *gao* branch could smack her
In the middle of her head
She would swear it is the god of thunder
But the god of thunder does not strike and leave the person alive
Yourid woman
What have I done to you
To make you wish my death
For peace to be
One cannot go beyond the hereafter
If the woman could go beyond the hereafter!

Unhappiness is not limited to the new wife. The first wife may be unhappy about the change in the family dynamics, and there might be an increase in jealousy among the wives caused by the husband, as described in this brief Jula song recorded by Derive (1986).

If you see that the women are jealous
It is the husband who provokes the jealousy
It is by putting the last in first place
That the husband has provoked jealousy.

Kabore Oger published two songs that deal with inequality in polygynous marriages. The experience of the women in such marriages is so well understood by all members of society that it has become a subject of songs sung by children. In this song recorded by Oger (1993:205–206), the situation of the unhappy wife is symbolized by the lower-quality straw on the roof of her house in comparison with the higher-quality straw called *zemtaaba*. In the second part of the song, the children assume the voice of Naare Yamma, who says that she will not return. The refusal of the woman to accept a role inferior to that of the favorite in both this song and the one that follows underscores the extent to which women's freedom to complain about a husband's behavior is recognized in society—even by children. The use of the French expression *mal aimée,* or unloved, is the wife's way of emphasizing her unhappy condition.

Naare Yamma, Naare Yamma
In the compound of Naare Yamma, there are many women
Now he takes this one and makes her his favorite

And he takes that one he makes her his *mal aimée*
The house of his *mal aimée* is roofed with ordinary straw
The house of his favorite is covered with *zemtaaba*.
Naare Yamma, Naare Yamma
I'm going to return to my father's house at Yogpeongo.
The people of Yogpeongo ask my news.
Moreover, if I go there, I will not come back.
Naare Yamma, Naare Yamma,
Naare Yamma, Naare Yamma.

In this second song recorded by Oger (1993:204), the man appears to play one wife against the other in a manner designed, according to the lyrics, to provoke conflict. *Sagbo* and *sauce potassé* are two kinds of dishes.

Provocation, I start again
Provocation, I start again the provocation
I say that the provocation, you start it again
I prepared for you *sagbo* and you ate it.
I prepared for you *sauce potassé* and you ate it.
I prepared porridge for you and you ate it.
And I heated up water for you and you washed yourself
And then you quickly got up to go warm yourself at the hearth of my co-wife.
I say provocateur, you are provoking [me].

A woman contemplating marriage may be concerned about the nature of the relationship with the man she may marry, or even about the entire concept of marriage. The Bamana song below comes from a corpus collected by Pascal Couloubaly in the village of NCòla, Mali, between 1981 and 1987. Here, the man comes in for criticism because of the way, in the eyes of the singer, he abandoned his first wife, his eldest son, and the wife of his older brother, who joined the family following the custom when an older brother of the husband dies. Couloubaly observes in a note that the supposed injustice of the father toward his eldest son is surprising, and wonders if the problem is that the wife wants to add more victims to her complaint and thus she implies that the father is too severe with the son (1990:29–30).

His truth does not please.
The truth of the abandoned wife does not please.
The abandoned wife is never right
The truth does not please
The truth of the abandoned wife does not please
To be abandoned cannot be right.

Who is the first
Who is the first unloved of the family?
She is not right
It is the first wife
It is the first wife of the home
To be abandoned is not right.

Who is the second
Who is the second unloved of the family?
He is not right
It is the eldest son
It is the eldest son of the family
To be abandoned cannot be right.

Who is the third
Who is the third unloved of the family?
She is not right
It is the inherited wife [the wife of the late older brother]
To be abandoned cannot be right.

In another song on the same theme (Couloubaly 1990:32), co-wives develop a modus vivendi that avoids jealousy between them. Speaking both to her co-wife and to her husband, the singer declares that competition for his attention no longer exists and that the two women now do as they want.

Hey, may my co-wife do what she wants
I have ceased to be a competitor
She doesn't care about it
And me too.

She made him a *culotte bouffante* [large baggy pants]
And me too!
Then a *grand boubou* [long caftan]
And me too!

Hey! May my co-wife do what she wants
I have ceased to be a competitor
She doesn't care about it.
And me too.

Household Management

In most parts of the Sahel both women and men contribute to the family income by working in agriculture and selling products—food, containers, clothing, etc.—in local markets. But because there is little work for men during the long dry season from October to May, some men try to augment the family income by migrating to coastal cities to find work. In the following Songhoy-Zarma song, recorded by Fatoumata-Agnès Diarra (1971:85), the singer warns her husband that he needs to go south to earn enough money to pay for the many family expenses, not only for their own nuclear family, but also for the extended family, including their parents, and for taxes. The tone of the woman's song suggests that she plays a significant role in the management of the family. The reference to the "child of the cool season" is to the man who stays at home rather than head south. The "bald head" alludes to the older generation of men who are no longer able to travel in search of jobs on the coast.

Child of the cool season with the flaking ankles
Who one might take for undercooked millet paste
The reason for remaining here during the cool season, you will regret.
The *boubou* of my father? You will pay for it.
His *boubou* and trousers, you will pay for them.
The wrapper of my mother? You will obtain it for her.
Her wrapper and her shoes, you will pay for them.
My own clothes, you will pay for them.
Hear the trumpet that announces the collection of taxes
Whether you have anything or not, you will pay for them.
Child of the cold with the bald head, you will pay for them.
This, for you who spends the cool season here, you will regret it.
Look at this head that resembles that of his father
These skinny legs that one would take for those of his father.
Ankles that one would take for undercooked millet paste
Hear then the trumpet that announces the collection of taxes
Whether or not you have anything, you will pay for them.

Separation and Divorce

In some cases, a woman finds herself in a situation where she feels as though she cannot win. If she escapes the marriage by the extraordinary means described below, she loses her status as a married woman. If she remains in the marriage in order to maintain her position, she suffers. The last line in the song underscores her predicament (Luneau 1981:156–157; 2010:123–124).

Ho, all the women.
Call the women.
I didn't know what it was to be a woman
If I had known it would be like that

I would have changed myself into a bird
In the bush
If I could not have changed myself into a bird
I would have changed myself into a doe
In the bush
To be married
Is misfortune
Not to be married is misfortune.

In the next song, recorded by Luneau (1981:128; 2010:43–44), the singer finds it almost impossible to reconcile her desire to meet her obligations as an obedient daughter with her unhappiness as a wife. She decides that there is only one solution to her dilemma.

This is not a refusal!
The marriage that my father and mother wanted
Was a blessed marriage
This is not a refusal!

This is not a refusal!
But maybe someday,
I would take the road to the big city
Nobody knows anything about it.

This is not a refusal!
But perhaps someday, here
At dawn
I will be dead.

This is not a refusal!
The marriage that my father and mother wanted
Was a blessed marriage
This is not a refusal!

When things do not turn out satisfactorily for a bride because of relations with the husband, a co-wife, or the family of the husband, the woman may ask her husband to take her back to her own family. In this song, she evokes their happy memories of their courtship and wedding when many gifts, including kola nuts, sheep, and cows, were received (Luneau 1981:143–144; 2010:115).

Take me back to my mother
Marriage no longer means anything
Take me back
Take me back

To the time when you were marrying me
Big kola nuts were coming and going
Take me back

At the time when you were marrying me
Good luck was coming and going
Take me back

When you were marrying me
Fat sheep were coming and going
Take me back

Take me back to my mother
Marriage no longer means anything
Take me back
Take me back

When you were marrying me
Good luck was coming and going
Take me back

At the time when you were marrying me
Fat cows came and went
Take me back

Take me back to my mother
Marriage no longer means anything
Take me back.

Diakité (2003) offers a similar but longer song that describes the cool welcome given to a woman who returns home after being beaten by her new husband.

Singer:
1. I tell you that there are many people in this world,
2. There are many people, but few of them can soften the heart of others.
3. Women, mothers, there are numerous people,
4. They are numerous, but few can soften the heart of others.
   Chorus:
5. Yes, there are plenty of people on this earth,
6. Plenty of people, but few people of tenderness!
   Singer:
7. Once upon a time, an orphan girl was married,
8. She was married by an unscrupulous man.
9. Her marriage didn't last long.
10. As soon as her wedding ceremony ended,

11. She always got violently beaten
12. By her husband and her in-laws: she was tied up and beaten!
13. She was obliged to go back to her native family,
14. The orphan girl had to return home.
15. Unfortunately for her again, she was not allowed to put her luggage down at home.
16. Her luggage of newly married woman [was] not welcome there.
17. There again, she was violently beaten.
18. She was forced back to her husband's home,
19. The girl returned back to her husband's home.
20. There again, she was received with [the] whip.
21. Once again, she went back to her own home.
22. When she arrived home again,
23. Her luggage [was] not welcome there,
24. Her luggage of newly married woman didn't get any place to be put.
25. She was shown the big vestibule to settle there,
26. That it was there the vestibule for married women who come back home.
27. The girl started weeping.
28. She told many bitter cursing words,
29. That for having stepped in the big vestibule,
30. That henceforth, every married woman who returns
31. Sleeps in the big vestibule like her,
32. That the one who fails to do so,
33. That the vestibule take away her soul.
34. And that became a pact,
35. And every married woman who returned back home,
36. Had to sleep in the vestibule.
37. That became a rule,
38. And all of them slept in the vestibule.
39. When they come for funerals,
40. They all sleep in the big vestibule.
41. When they come for excision ceremonies,
42. They all sleep in the big vestibule.
43. Women, mothers, there are many people in this world,
44. But those who have a sympathetic heart are very few!

In the following song (Luneau 1981:145; 2010:116), the singer appeals to three men with the power to help her, the *commandant de cercle* (chief administrator for the region), her father, and a griot, who may have played a key role in the negotiations for the marriage. Given the references to her father in the song, it appears that she may have called her father before the *commandant* with the griot as her witness. The closing lines are charged with irony as she describes the best fathers.

> Papa commandant, my father,
> Respected griot.
> I am determined to divorce.
>
> If you do not speak
> To the father who gave me life
> I am going to give myself
> To the hippopotamus in the river
> So that he can make of me
> His noon meal.
>
> That will be better for my father
> He is an excellent father
> Who shortens the life of his children
> Who shortens the life of his children.

Another reason for divorce is trickery on the part of the husband, which is the case in a long 1,056-line narrative by Safi Hassane, recorded by Sidikou in Niamey, Niger, in July 1995. It is in the genre of the *saabi,* literarily "being grateful." The genre is "viewed as an epic for women," explains Sidikou (2001:144), or as a *deeda,* a term for a long narrative. A *saabi* may focus on the wedding night, the arrival of a new wife, or when a woman gives birth to a child. In this particular narrative, one finds a variety of examples of the situations of newly-wed women. Sidikou explains that the *saabi* reveals "how these African women think" and serves as a kind of "cultural barometer" (143).

Toward the end of this particular *saabi,* a man and a woman get married. After the wedding, and at the beginning of the rainy season, the couple goes to the field to plant, the man walking ahead and making holes with his hoe, the woman following with a calabash of seeds. She is supposed to drop a few seeds in each hole and then cover them. After the couple returns from the field, the man announces that he plans to divorce his wife. The outcome reveals that the woman is more clever than the man. In the narrative, the reference to a divorce paper may seem to be an anachronism in rural Africa, but it reflects the fact that a marriage is sometimes sealed by a document delivered by a marabout, or religious leader. In this case, the term *tira* (paper) *how* (tie up) indicates that the narrator has obtained the document from either a local marabout where she lives or in a city of Niger, and therefore a divorce requires a formal reversal of this process. The text below is an excerpt from the much longer narrative.

935   Now she took the calabash of millet
      She placed the one containing the sowing seeds in it
      Her husband was carrying the hoe on his shoulder
      They were chatting
      They were going to the farm.
940   The husband tilled,
      She took the millet
      You know you use a calabash
      To sow
      She sowed from near to far
945   She was closing the empty holes
      When she reached a spot
      She dumped the millet
      In just one hole
      Then she went back for more millet
950   They sowed all day long, all day long
      Until dusk when they came back home to sleep
      The next morning
      They went back for the remaining land
      By noon they finished the farm
955   They came back home, they bathed
      They were resting
      They were chatting
      Her husband told her,
      He said, "You see the mother of the house."
960   He said, "By Allah, you see,
      Now the relationship has come to an end.
      Everything stops here where our Lord
      Has put an end to it.
      Here is your divorce paper
965   You should just leave your house."
      She said, "No."
      He said, "Yes."
      She said, "I will not leave your house."
      He said, "It is a lie.
970   As for me, a woman has never sowed together with me
      And done the rainy season work with me once."
      She laughed and said,
      "You did not divorce me first,
      I first divorced you."

975 He said, "No, you are lying
You just do not want to leave."
She said, "By Allah I am leaving,
But I had divorced you first.
Only you did not realize it
980 I had already divorced you.
And I am obtaining revenge for all the women you have already deceived."
A man with his tricks
Any trick a man has out of wickedness
If a man thinks he has ten tricks
985 One trick from a woman will outplay his.
She said, "Consider three days,
On the fourth day,
You well know that it is the time one
Goes out to check one's land
990 To see the new shoots?"
She said, "Go to your farm that day."
She said, "You would know that day that I was the one who divorced you first."
The woman gathered her belongings and left
On the third day everybody went to check the farm
995 The man went to his farm
Bad news! He sat and wailed
His friends' shoots were going *fararara* [onomatopoeia for growing]
As for this one, when he looks out
He sees the shoots in one spot
1000 Now this side has nothing
So, of these two people
It was said before that by Allah the
Man was really wicked
Because he divorced wives
1005 This one divorced nine
This one divorced eight,
It was the woman indeed who got him
The woman is the one who divorced nine husbands
The man divorced eight wives
1010 So you see the one [her] with nine outdid the other
Because she knew how to trick him
That is why the polemic goes on.
It is said by Allah that whatever
A man can do,

1015 A woman knows how to trick better.
    A deceiving and nasty man
    And whatever you do out of wickedness
    A woman can definitely outdo you
    Because she has many tricks.

2 ⟶ Children

It is difficult to overstate the importance of children for women in the Sahel region of West Africa—or, for that matter, anywhere else in the world.

FERTILITY AND STERILITY

Once married and integrated as best she can into the new family, a woman's focus shifts to having a child. To fail to have a child is to fail as a woman and as a wife. It may lead to pressure by the family for the husband to take a second wife who might be more fertile. If the second wife cannot have a child, then attention may shift to the husband's inability to impregnate his wives.

In Jola society in Senegal, a woman who has no children, or who has lost her children, is seen as the victim of evil spirits. She must therefore undergo a *kanyalen* ritual that will transform her into an *anyalen,* a different kind of woman who takes a new name, wears different clothing, and adopts behavior that reflects her status. This particular way of responding to the lack of children requires some explanation. Langeveld (2003), who collected a series of *kanyalen* songs, reports:

> A group of women, a man, or a mask association now has responsibility for her. In general, it is not the woman who makes the decision to become *anyalena. . . .* Usually, the women of the village decide that one of their number has lost too many children and that action should be taken. The initiation ritual often takes her by surprise: she is brought to the initiation place under false pretenses. She has to be deceived because the status of *anyalena* is not at all attractive. . . . An important aspect of her identity transformation is expressed in her conduct. From the moment she is initiated as an *anyalena,* she has to change her behavior: at rituals she is expected to be the passage-maker (the first and last to dance), she has to be provocative, break sexual taboos, and sometimes be childish. She has to compose songs to be sung during rituals. . . . The only source of power the *anyalena* has is her creativity in expressing her frustration about her powerless position.

The themes in the songs of the *anyalena* range from criticizing her own conduct to making accusations about men. What they have in common is that they make allusion to her fate and her powerlessness.

> Entré, her brother, asks, she is ill, how is she?
> She says that she does not work in the house
> She does not have children, she does not have anything.
> One can send her with the ferry-boat to Affiniam, she can stay there
>   because she possesses nothing.
> Her mother asks also what she is doing,
> She says that she is doing nothing because she does not have anything
> She can send her with the ferry-boat, and leave her there.

If the wife and her husband are able to conceive a child, the birth validates the mother's membership in the sisterhood of women. A child indicates her femininity and her capacity to give life. If the child is a boy in a patrilineal society, the woman often earns greater appreciation in the eyes of her husband and her in-laws because he offers the promise that the family lineage will continue to new generations. Finally, the birth of a child strengthens the link between the mother and her own family.

HAVING CHILDREN

The following Bamana song recorded by Luneau in the town of Beleko, Mali, during 1967–1968 (1981:97–98; 2010:80) is typical of the value attached to children.

> The child one brings into the world
> The child one brings into the world
> The child one brings into the world
> Is a jewel
> Yes, even if you put golden earrings on the ears of your wife
> It is the child
> Who is the jewel of the woman.

BIRTH

When a young woman experiences her first pregnancy, in some societies in the Sahel she may return to the home of her parents a few months prior to the birth of her child in order to benefit from the care and support of her family, especially her female relatives. By rejoining her family, the mother is also able to avoid intimacy with her husband at a time when she is fully focused on the challenges of pregnancy.

Although motherhood is considered a blessing, society also recognizes that delivering a child is an ordeal for a woman. The expectant mother is pampered at her mother's home during this time and nourished with specially cooked food to help her gain strength and energy. In communities where fattening is practiced (see below under "Beauty"), she is given extra food after the birth to increase her body mass before she goes back to her husband.

The actual birth is as difficult in Africa as anywhere else—and the woman and those around her do not often have the same facilities that one normally finds in industrialized countries. In the song below, typically sung by the midwife, the goal, explains Amadou Hampaté Bâ (1999:3–4), was to help the future mother "bear the blows the baby was dealing to her belly with head, hands, and feet, trying to break free from the cocoon that prevented it from being its own master." Numerous times, the midwife appeals to Nyakaruba, the goddess of maternity.

Wuy way o! Nyakaruba, push hard!
Childbirth is laborious, Nyakaruba
Giving birth to a boy is laborious
Nyakaruba,
Push hard!
Waay waayo! Nyakaruba, push hard!
Childbirth is laborious, Nyakaruba
Nyakaruba.
Push hard!
Eeh, eeh, Nyakaruba! Push hard!
Childbirth is laborious, Nyakaruba
Giving birth to twins is laborious
Nyakaruba
Push hard!
Push hard all possible childbirths on earth, Nyakaruba
Push hard!
Push hard this very childbirth,
Nyakaruba, push it hard.

The mother usually does all she can to go through the delivery without conveying the stress that she is experiencing. In some communities, the show of emotion during childbirth—for example, cries of pain—may prompt songs to expose what is seen as shameful behavior.

The infant's survival depends in part on the quality of care it receives. The prospective mother needs all the help, wisdom, and education in child raising that society can provide—not simply from her own mother but also from other experienced women, who can take care of her throughout the pregnancy and sometimes for days or months afterward. This support eases the stress of pregnancy and birth. It also helps to lessen the impact of postpartum depression, a subject rarely discussed in these societies.

The successful birth of a child often leads to a celebration, including ceremonies and rituals for both the mother and the child. Both are celebrated through songs, incantations, and other expressions of joy. A song in Soninké recorded by Ousmane Diagana (1990:22) is sung after the birth of the child. The message here emphasizes the future of the child as a positive reflection not only of the family, but also of the society he or she represents.

> A child has seen the light of day at Diahounou
> When he grows up what a prodigy he will be
> A child has seen the day at Diahounou
> A newborn has seen the day at Diahounou
> When he grows up what a prodigy he will be.

NAMING

The naming of a child soon after birth links the child to the past as well as to particular events. The child may be named for an ancestor or, in some cases, for an event or for a quality desired by the parents. For the brief Jula song that follows, Derive (1986:1190) explains that the child was given the prestigious name of Fa Tiéba, the father of the founder of the kingdom of Kong in Côte d'Ivoire. Derive points out that the name represents both the most significant ancestor from the social perspective and high expectations for the child.

> Hey, one has given today the name of our ancestor
> That pleases us.
> Hey, one has given today the name of Tiéba,
> That pleases us.

The naming ceremony is a time of great celebration and attracts not only friends and relatives, but also griots and griottes eager to celebrate the heritage of the child. These professionals expect to be rewarded by the mother and her family and also by others in attendance for the songs of praise they sing during and after the naming ceremony. The following well-known song, explains Janson (2003:20–21), was sung by Jelinyama Jobarteh in Kanteh Kunda, the compound of a blacksmith family in the village of Manneh Kunda, near Basse in the Gambia. During the performance, she played a percussion rod called the *neo,* which is a short metal pipe struck by a large nail or similar piece of metal. In the song, adds Janson, the reference to "donate yourself" refers both to the actual gift and to the term *togo,* signifying "name" or "reputation." Two drums are cited in the song: the *junjung,* which is "beaten during ceremonies," and the *tuballou,* or "holy drum," which is beaten to announce "events associated with the Islamic calendar or during very important occasions." The drums indicate that the relatives on each side are very important, with various interpretations linking them to religious leaders, griots, and kings.

> Oh mother of the newborn, donate yourself
> New mother, donate yourself
> Oh mother of the newborn, donate yourself
> The lucky mother of the newborn, donate yourself
> Oh mother of the newborn, donate yourself
> New mother, donate yourself
> Some come into the world and depart from it
> without celebrating their child's naming ceremony
> They do not give anything to the Lord who created them
> Ah Adama's mother, donate yourself
> That is the truth
> Mother of the newborn with the pleasing name
> Praise be to God
> Oh mother of the newborn, donate yourself
> New mother, donate yourself
> Some people give plenty to the griots in Mande
> I do not expect that from the patrons of the griots in Mande
> Your mother's side is *junjung*
> Your father's side is *tuballou*
> You are the one related to Majula Konjira
> If you don't know
> A mean patron does not appreciate *jaliyaa*
> Being the griot of a person who does not have anything is not enjoyable
> Majula's Sira, you are not born to suffer
> Her mother's prayers have been answered
> She is the one related to Nfali Malang
> She is the one related to Maamudu Malang
> May God bless her with a long life
> May God give you many like this
> May God weaken the evil half-brothers
>
> Oh mother of the newborn, donate yourself
> New mother, donate yourself
> Oh mother of the newborn, donate yourself
> New mother, donate yourself.

Because of the commonality of experience among women and the fluidity in boundaries between families, the casual observer might not at first notice the difference between a biological mother and other mothers. The many tasks that fall on women, especially in rural areas, make it difficult for a biological mother to take care of her children alone. But a tradition based on community spirit and the contributions of groups of women, both within a family and in the larger village context, helps mothers to cope with the challenges of child care. Aunts, sisters, friends, grandmothers, co-wives, and neighbors are all involved. With this support, the mother can take care of her children, do household chores, and in many cases contribute to the economic needs of the family through a variety of commercial activities, such as selling agricultural produce and handicrafts in local markets. But it is difficult to replace the mother when the child needs to be helped to sleep.

LULLABIES

The Wolof song titled "Beeyoo Beeyoo" was recorded by George Joseph on March 5, 2002, in the village of Lambene, Senegal. The performance includes both a soloist (*debbe*) and a chorus (*awu*). The recurring lines convey the kind of repetition designed to lull a child to sleep. We have followed here Joseph's division of the poem into numbered strophes to permit an easier comparison with the original transcription, which can be found in the appendix.

1. *Solo*
Billy goat, goat, billy, billy
Oh me, my child is crying
Ayo billy.

2. *Chorus*
Billy goat, goat, billy, billy,
Oh me, my child is crying
Ayo billy.

3. *Solo*
Billy goat, goat, billy, billy
Oh me, my child is crying
Ayo billy.

4. *Chorus*
Billy goat, goat, billy, billy,
Oh me, my child is crying
Ayo billy.

5. *Solo*
Oh me my child
If he wants, he can cry
Mbakhar Birame
Billy goat, goat, billy, billy.

6. *Chorus*
Billy goat, goat, billy, billy
Oh me, my child is crying
Ayo billy

7. *Solo*
Talla my baby
If he wants, he can cry
Mbakhar Birame
Billy goat, goat, little, billy.

8. *Chorus*
Billy goat, goat, billy, billy,
Oh me, my child is crying
Ayo billy

9. *Solo*
Mali Coumba Dior
Déguène Fara Lamb
Sa Ndiouki younger daughter of Dior
You, why are you crying?
Talla my child, I do not want anything that hurts him.
Billy, billy.

10. *Chorus*
Billy goat, goat, billy, billy,
Oh me, my child is crying
Ayo billy.

11. *Solo*
Talla Gouy my child
May god make you a grandfather
Mbakhar Birame
Billy goat, goat, little, billy

12. *Chorus*
Billy goat, goat, billy, billy,

Oh me, my child is crying
Ayo billy.

13. *Solo*
You are my one and only
Because of you I no longer ask
Mbakhar Birame
Billy, billy, mother ayo billy.

14. *Chorus*
Billy goat, goat, billy, billy,
Oh me, my child is crying
Ayo billy.

15. *Solo*
Talla de Ndongo Faal ici
If he wants he can be spoiled
Because he is a nobleman
Ayo, ayo, billy, billy.

16. *Chorus*
Billy goat, goat billy, billy
O me, my child is crying.
Ayo billy.

17. *Solo*
Talla de Bagne Ngoné, Déguène
I do not know why you cry
Mbakhar Birame
Billy goat, goat, little, billy

18. *Chorus*
Billy goat, goat, billy, billy,
Oh me, my child is crying
Ayo billy.

19. *Solo*
Baye Fall who is at Kosso
If you want you can be spoiled
Mbakhar Birame
Billy-o! a pity
Ayo billy.

20. *Chorus*
Billy goat, goat, billy, billy,
Oh me, my child is crying
Ayo billy.

21. *Solo*
Oh me, my child is crying
I am walking around with him
Billy, billy, mother, ayo billy.

22. *Chorus*
Billy goat, goat, billy, billy,
Oh me, my child is crying
Ayo billy.

In the following Toucouleur (Fulbe) song, published by Issa Kane in 1932 in a journal for teachers in West Africa (99), the collector explains that the singer adds the rhythm of gently patting a sick child on the bottom. The combination of the repeated tapping and the repetition of the words may increase the soporific influence of the song.

Bilil bôli bili bayna
Bilil bôli bili bayna
You drank some milk
And you vomit some butter

O bayna ô bay
O bayna ô bay
Your mother went to the jujube tree
She picked a jujube
She ate it in the middle of the river
O bayna ô bay
O bayna ô bay

EDUCATION

The term *education* normally refers to attendance at a formal school, but in many parts of Africa and, indeed, around the globe, education includes the acquisition of knowledge about the world, about society, and above all about appropriate individual behavior. Education begins at home with the parents, but as the child becomes older, other adults in society contribute to educating children—for example, relatives and artisans such as griots, griottes, and blacksmiths. These two groups often play roles in one of the most important aspects of education: initiation into adulthood. This may include not only narratives about the past but also circumcision for boys and excision for girls, a practice that generates debate both in Africa and outside of the continent. As Thiaw points out for Serer initiation traditions, excision is part of a much larger process of education involving a secret association of women in which fertility, conception, birth, and other topics of concern are explained to the young as they mature.

One of the songs recorded by Thiaw (2005:178) alludes both to the importance of the mother-daughter tie in the larger world of women—and hence the importance for the daughter of meeting her mother's expectations—and to the educational process (involving maxims, stories, and other forms of cultural information) that will prepare her to face life's challenges into old age. The metaphor of dew at the end underscores the beauty of virtue but also the ease with which it can disappear.

> O Ginaan daughter of Yande
> Such is the custom
> Ginaan daughter of Yande
> I am going to speak to you
> Ginaan daughter of Yande
> I am going to speak to you of the true wisdom of today
> Ginaan daughter of Yande
> I will tell you the stories today
> Ginaan daughter of Yande
> I would tell you many things today
> Ginaan daughter of Yande
> I am happy about the drums
> Ginaan daughter of Yande
> At the hour of the dance at Pelew
> Ginaan daughter of Yande
> I ask God
> That he lead you to old age
> Ginaan daughter of Yande
> I am going to talk to you about old age
> Ginaan daughter of Yande
> I am going to talk with you about wisdom
> Ginaan daughter of Yande
> Do you know that the sacred forest is the custom

Ginaan daughter of Yande
I have spoken to you of maxims
Ginaan daughter of Yande
Life is a dew
Ginaan daughter of Yande
Do you know that dew
Ginaan daughter of Yande
If you bump it it falls
Ginaan daughter of Yande
I thank the women of Pelew
Ginaan daughter of Yande

An important part—but not the only event—in the preparation of girls to become women is often excision, which is a form of genital cutting. For the girl who does not complete this part of her initiation into adulthood, the result is shame, as described in the following song from the 1967–1968 Beleko corpus recorded by Luneau (1974:452–453; 2010:29).

Little Ayira cried
We le le le
Little Ayira cried
People of Nygolokouna
Little Ayira cried.

She crossed the river
She passed the pond
A ram sacrificed, an old chicken

She arrived near a woman
A woman who was winnowing millet
Woman, aren't you waiting for me?

At the sound of the knife
At the sound of the knife that excised
The little Ayira escaped

To crouch and to get up
The only day that that can be done
To crouch and to get up
Man! The noble race has escaped.

To get down on the knees and to get up
The only day that that can be done

To get down on the knees and to get up
Man! The noble race has escaped.

LAMENTATIONS ABOUT CHILDREN

There are many reasons for mothers to be concerned about the welfare of their children, but the most common is illness and, in some cases, the death of a child from a disease, accident, or war. Until recently, in many regions of Africa there was a 50 percent chance of a child dying before the age of five from disease. For some women, the loss of children exceeds this rate considerably. The high chance of a child dying is one of the reasons that families want to have as many children as possible, although the rate of fertility is declining in many areas as a result of improvements in health care. But a large number of children is still considered to be a form of wealth. If one child does not succeed, perhaps one or two of the others will, and later they will be able to take care of the parents. When a child is weaned or sick, or when the mother passes away, other members of the family hasten to help with advice and care. The first source of medical help and advice is often a traditional healer.

In this song from the Jula people of the Casamance region in southern Senegal, recorded by El Hadji Sagna (1986–1987:134–135), the chorus echoes the thoughts of the distraught mother who has lost more than one of her children to illness. At the same time, the singers convey a sense of community solidarity during this difficult time. The fact that this song was performed by a singer and a chorus suggest that it conveys not the actual situation of a woman who has lost a child, but instead was heard in a larger social context—for example, a ceremony where models of different kinds of songs were sung to express a mother's concern about one of the most challenging of her many burdens.

SINGER: My own misfortune is enigmatic. It harvests without respite my children.
CHORUS: I say that I do not know how this happened to me, to me!
SINGER: When Fanta arrived, I told her to sweep the compound, we will then show it to our friends so that they will help us to identify the disease. When Sanana arrived, she told me, "Go to Katinong, there, show it to Mamadou Bâ so that he can give you a medicine to take."
    I applied the prescribed treatment, and then I went to look for food to eat, it is then that I noticed that the pain became worse. I went back to see him. He said to me, "Brave woman, how are you?"
CHORUS: I told him, "It has become worse, help me again."
SINGER: He said to me, "Now, brave woman, how are you?"

CHORUS: I told him, "It has become worse, help me again."
  I told him, "It has become worse, help me again."
  I told him, "It has become worse, help me again."
SINGER: My own misfortune.

Another far more complex lamentation about the loss of a child appears in one of the first recorded and published songs performed by a woman from the Sahel. It was collected by the well-known colonial administrator Jules Brévié in 1915 and published in Dakar in 1918 (217–222). The transcription and translation into French appeared to be linguistically accurate, according to Kassim Koné, a Malian scholar familiar with the history of the region where the events took place.

Brévié's goal was evidently to give great attention to a song that could be interpreted as support for the French colonial mission. To understand the deeper meaning of the lyrics, however, one must separate the local context from the co-opting of the song by the French administrator for an entirely different purpose.

A woman named D'Namba Kouloubali from the village of Massantola in Mali lost her only son in a battle between a French-led force and two rebelling African leaders, Diossé and Samba. Although the song is a long lamentation, it also contains political criticism of the two leaders who chose, she believes, the wrong time and conditions to challenge the French.

In the song, one hears the voices of the grieving mother and of Diossé, one of the rebels, as conveyed by the mother and the chorus of sisters, who offer their solidarity to her.

The old woman:
Diossé lost the men uselessly.
Where did you leave your men?
Where did you leave your warriors?

Diossé:
Leave me alone. I tried to get out of this difficult situation.
Go ask the whites.
Go ask their soldiers.
Go look at the edge of the dry swamp.

The old woman:
Diossé didn't flee, but he lost his reputation.
Samba fled, the whites are brave.
Samba was afraid.
Samba of Massantola is not a man!

The sisters:
Samba and Diossé unleashed a war for no reason.
They had our elders killed uselessly.

The old woman:
I no longer have a son, I will have nothing more to eat.
I will have no more clothing . . . and I am old.

The sisters:
Old woman, don't cry.
We'll marry, we'll nourish you.
Don't cry, we'll watch out for you.
Let go of Samba and Diossé, they are evildoers.

3 —❧ *Women in Society*

In contrast to the stereotype of women confined to the domestic sphere, songs about women in society give a different picture. Women participate in the difficult work of growing food. They may comment on politics and exhort their sisters to become involved at every level of society. One genre that conveys many of these topics is praise and criticism of other women and men. Finally, they are concerned with appropriate behavior, sports, beauty, health, and death.

WORK

Across the Sahel, women are widely viewed as working harder than men because they must not only take care of the children, but also participate in a variety of other tasks. They play a central role in agriculture, planting their own gardens and helping in the fields, as seen in the song above about the woman who tricked her husband. Whatever they do, they must work under the same conditions as men, including the high heat of the sun. If the sky is often overcast during the season of the harmattan in January through March, by contrast, the planting season in May and June is a time of great heat diminished only occasionally by the clouds and resulting coolness that accompany all-too-rare rainstorms.

In addition to their direct roles in agricultural work, women also contribute indirectly by singing invocations for rain and by exhorting men who are clearing fields or harvesting grain, as in the following two Soninké songs recorded by Diagana (1990:247–249).

> If there were a little shade in the sky
> If there were a little milk in the gourd
> If there were a little *singuété* [millet and milk porridge] in the calabash.
> The plowing would be more pleasant
> The ploughing in mid-morning would be pleasant
> The ploughing woud be pleasant.
> The ploughing in the summer would be more agreeable.

We call for the help of Allah
We ask for aid from the angel Gabriel, the generous one
So that the shoots coming out of the soil may grow.

We have millet
The millet that God was kind enough to give us
But there is a lack of water to prepare it.

We call for the help of Allah
We ask for aid from the angel Gabriel, the generous one.

We cry for our grandmother
Grandmother is dead, we need water to wash her body for her burial.
We cry for our grandmother, we need water to wash her body for her burial.

May the rain fall *diour*
May the rain of the vast sky fall *diour*
The rain and its *digui dikkou* [onomatopoeia for the sound of thunder]
The rain and its *daga-dakkou* [onomatopoeia for the sound of rain].

The rain and its great gourds

We'll have our little calabashes
Our little calabashes for string beans
Our little calabashes for sorrel
Our little calabashes for wild fonio [type of small millet].
May the rain fall *diour*
May the rain from the vast sky fall *diour*.

POLITICS

Women are widely viewed as leaving politics to men and concerning themselves with domestic affairs and agricultural work. But in the Wolof *taasu,* or
praise song, below, recorded by Lisa McNee at a political rally on April 25, 1993,
women from Louga, a town and region in northwest Senegal, "expressed their
opinion about the aid to [Senegalese] refugees from Mauritania." These people
had been forced to flee Mauritania after a border dispute between the two
countries in 1989. During an election campaign four years later, some women
had not forgotten these events. McNee explains that the song "both praised
and criticized" the ruling party and its government, led by Abdou Diouf. Their
complaint is that the president of Senegal talks but does not act, although this
is better than the actions of the president of Mauritania, Ould Taya, in whose
country Senegalese were murdered and tortured with apparent government
approval. The women in subtle and indirect fashion, especially indicated by

their subdued tone during the political rally where they sang, are also criticizing Diouf for not doing enough for them. McNee concludes that these Senegalese women are "taking an authority otherwise denied to them . . . by linking
the personal to the political" in the song below. The last line, indicating that
Diouf is better than Taya because he does not kill, implies that his superiority
is quite limited. Yes, he does not kill, but what does he do to settle the complex
differences between the two countries and to address the claims of those who
have suffered on the Senegalese side of the border? The reference to Kumba
Dem, the mother of Abdou Diouf, is a reminder that he is rooted in his family
and has obligations to them and to society in general.

> I say Abdou Diouf
> If it weren't for that Kumba Dem's child
> We'd have died in Mauritania
> No one took us in.
>
> I say Abdou Diouf!
> If it weren't for him
> We'd have died, all of us
> No one saved us
> Oh, Abdou Diouf—rescue!
>
> Abdou Diouf
> I prefer you to Ould Taya
> Who walks and kills.
>
> I say Abdou Diouf
> You are different from Ould Taya
> Who walks and kills.

Songs about the public sphere of politics reflect a growing sense of independence in many cultures in the Sahel. For example, in the 1990s, Tuareg women
began to sing about the rebellions against the governments of Mali and Niger.
Susan Rasmussen, an anthropologist who has collected songs from the Tuareg
in northern Niger as part of a wider research program, has come across songs
of a political nature rooted in the continuing campaign of the Tuareg peoples
for greater autonomy. She explains, "Many Tuareg singers now also incorporate
themes of wider political resistance into their verses, thereby forging 'feminism' into a united front of Tuareg nationalism with men." In some of their
songs, women have shifted from lyrics about love to wider concerns about cultural autonomy. They are going "beyond gendered themes of relations between
the sexes, toward merging with wider issues of political nationalism and cultural revitalization, thereby confirming, in some respects, other observations

regarding globalization and feminism." Rasmussen explains that "women are recognized by most local men as fully equal in terms of their competence. Women and men alike tell stories of a few female rebels who performed heroic deeds during the rebellion, an echo of songs about earlier heroes" (Rasmussen 2003).

Although we have placed this song under the rubric of politics, it would also fit well in the category of "belief" because it is performed during a *tende n goumaten,* or possession ceremony. The song was recorded in northern Niger in January 2002. The words in brackets were inserted by Rasmussen. The names are pseudonyms to protect the identities of the subjects.

> Oh, young girls, if you know God
> you must assist with the festivities, the festivities have become orphaned
> This song I have composed for the young people
> Who formerly served in the rebellion
> Who were born in Niger, those who made
> The rain of iron at dawn.
> The missile that roars like a lion, the Kalashnikov that shoots
> Young people, I thank you for taking up arms
> on the shoulders.
> I tell you
> Me, I tell you
> *Tchihoulene yighwan* Moussa, Silimane,
> My greetings for you Mamane, Souley,
> And Kadou, Ahoulou, Kadi,
> Kadou, I encourage you, Sidi, who saved [helped] a thousand persons.

ORGANIZING

Another way that women manifest their presence in society is singing to promote organizations. The song below is in praise of a women's association (Mack 2004:221–223) and was composed in written form in 1967 by Hawa Gwaram. But before turning to the lyrics, it is important to point out that one of the particularities of Hausa songs and poetry is that the border between the two is porous. Mack points out, "Part of the problem for the researcher is Hausa terminology for the two genres. *Wa'ka* (pl. *wa'ko'ki*) is the Hausa term for a broad range of works from poetry to declamation, all of which is normally sung or chanted. The term is not readily translated, but comprises a range of meanings in English from song to written verse. To the Hausa, however, it is all 'song'" (Mack 2003).

This song offers many different perspectives on the roles of women. It includes a catalog of the kinds of jobs that women hold in the highly patriarchal society of northern Nigeria and a listing of the good works of the association for the needy in the region. Finally, it reveals that women know how to use their strength to obtain support from men, and it cites the donations of one male leader in order, it seems, to shame other men into donating to the women's society.

Song for the Association of Women of the North

1. In the name of God, I will compose a song
   About the solidarity of women in the north
2. I invoke God's aid, may he increase my insight
3. People of Kano, we ask your support
   May you help us, women northerners
4. Many people are asking me
   The reason for an association in the north
5. I want to enlighten everyone
   So that they will know about the association of the north
6. We are helping them with their occupational skills
   So that they needn't wander about worthless in the north
7. We have come together to help each other
   Together with the women of the north
8. Authorities of Kano, we ask that you
   Show us the way for the women of the north
9. We pool our money for the welfare of
   The association of women of the north
10. We pool our possessions because of friendship
    Among the women of the north
11. There are those with money and those who teach
    In the association of women of the north
12. There are market sellers in the association
    And common people in the association of northerners
13. There are those who teach reading
    In Hausa and English in the northern association
14. We teach weaving shirts and hats
    And sewing by machine in the northern association
15. We teach child care and hygiene
    We teach cooking to northerners
16. We teach the art of conversation and headscarf tying
    We teach proper behavior to the northerners
17. There are those who want to join the association
    Who are afraid of the women of the north
18. If you come to us, join without fear
    Come to the association of the north

19. It will cost you thirty kobo [seven cents] to join
    And sixpence for a card for northerners

20. From the association no one is excluded
    Come to the association of the women of the north

21. There are the affluent and those from government
    In the association of northern women

22. There are teachers in our association
    And ordinary folks in the association

23. There is no discrimination between us
    In the association of women of the north

24. We pool our money to help ourselves
    And for our freedom, women of the north

25. We make purchases and take them to the orphans
    In the association of women of the north

26. We make purchases and take them to the orphans
    We give them to the destitute women of the north

27. We buy a television by ourselves and take it to the soldiers
    At the Kano hospital—that's the help of the northerners

28. We buy bicycles with association money
    and take them to the orphans of the women of the north

29. We buy towels and plastic bags and blankets
    We buy milk for the orphans of the north

30. Well, now we have our own land
    We will begin building, women of the north

31. The Kano magistrate, the governor, the district officer
    And the emir, please help the women of the north

32. Governor of Kano, Alhaji Audu Bako,
    Has helped us, the association of the north

33. He gave us four bales of cloth, it's true
    to give to the destitute from the women of the north

34. When we divided the cloth into nine piles
    We took it to the countryside to help the northerners

35. Our leader is Hajiya Ladi Bako
    With her and other ethnic groups of women of the north

36. We went to the Mil Tara hospital and gave them things
    To Shahuci, the place for destitute northerners

37. To Kumbotso, Bichi, and Ungogo and to
    Yadakunya—we went to the place of the northerners

38. We went to Wudil, even to Dawakin Tofa
    We gave to the destitute from the women of the north

39. May God give us good fortune
    May he give us the things we want in the north
40. The association of Kano, with the self-help that was done
    Gave us 800 naira [US$150] for the women of the north
41. The community department of the L. G. A. [local government
    authority] of Kano
    Gave us 300 naira [US$60] for the women of the north
42. There are four or five I cannot name
    Who have helped us
43. Well, people, every one of you
    Come to the association of women of the north
44. Let us praise the northerners
    Let us exalt the members of the association of the women of the north
45. It is ended, with praise to God, here I'll cut short
    The song of the women's association of the north
46. If anyone asks you who wrote this song
    About the women in the association of the north
47. It is I, Hawa Gwaram, who composed this song
    on women in the association of the north.
    Thanks be to God.

Praise, or *yabo* in Hausa, is expressed for individual women and for women in general and their capacity to contribute to society. This song, composed orally, was recorded by Mack from Binta Katsina on March 22, 1980 (2004:157–159), and offers a powerful exhortation to the women of Nigeria to take a more active role both in the diverse workforce of the country and in the government. The singer's method is to list the many different jobs women can do, thus providing evidence "through a variety of suggestions" for what Mack describes as "women's unlimited professional potential" (119). Implicit in the singer's claim, given the checkered history of the country's government, is that women can do a better job than men.

Song for the Women of Nigeria

1   God, our Lord, our Prophet, God's messenger
     Help the women of Nigeria
     God, our Lord, our Prophet, God's messenger
     Assist the women of Nigeria
5   Women of Nigeria
     Women of Nigeria
     You will do every kind of work

Women of Nigeria
Women of Nigeria
10   You should try to understand
You could do every kind of work
I'm giving you an office, women—you can do office work
Women of Nigeria, you will do every kind of work
You should be given the chance to take charge
15   You can do the office work
You can do administrative work
You should be given the chance to take charge, to try, women of Nigeria
You can do all of the typists' jobs
You know people, daughters of Nigeria
20   Women of Nigeria, you could do every kind of work
You should do every kind of work
Women of Nigeria, you could be in the offices
You can do paperwork
You can do paperwork
25   Women of Nigeria, you could take charge of the schools
Women of Nigeria, you could take charge of the schools and control them
You could be ministers in politics
Women of Nigeria, you could do every kind of work
You could do any kind of work
30   Here, women of Nigeria, you could do the typists' work
You could do the typing
Women of Nigeria, you should do every kind of work
Which kind of boasting will they do?
Men, which kind of boasting will they do?
35   You can do all the paperwork
You can be in the office
You can hold the pen
Well, what kind of boasting will they do?
Men, what kind of boasting will they do?
40   Women of Nigeria
Let's give you the chance to take charge
Women of Nigeria, let's give you the chance to take charge
You can become the government
Women of Nigeria
45   You can do the paperwork
You can do all the typing

Women of Nigeria
You can do all the typing
Women of Nigeria
50   What kind of boasting will you do?
Men, what kind of boasting will you do?
They can be in the office,
Give them a chair of their own,
Give them a chair of their own,
55   Women of Nigeria
Let's give you a chair of your own
Women of Nigeria
You could do every kind of work
You can drive cars, you can run machines
60   You can fly airplanes
Women of Nigeria
Thanks to the women of Nigeria. They've paid us and we thank them.
Thanks to the women of Nigeria. They've paid us and we thank them.
Hey, daughters of Nigeria
65   Hey, daughters of Nigeria
Thanks to the daughters of Nigeria
Hey, daughters of Nigeria, you should do every kind of work
You should do every kind of work, you should know every kind of work
You can write papers, you can pound the typewriter
70   You can fly airplanes
You know how to be in the office
You could do government work
And you could be police officers
You could do the customs work
75   Let's give you the chance to take charge
Women of Nigeria
Women of Nigeria, you know every kind of work,
You could do every kind of work
And you could do all kinds of work
80   God knows, women of Nigeria
You can be loving and obedient, I tell you, daughters of Nigeria
You can be loving and obedient, I tell you, daughters of Nigeria.
I say to you out there, Nigerians
We praise with thanks and blessings
85   I say to you, daughters of Nigeria, we praise with thanks and blessings.

SPORTS

Although we have not come across songs that portray women engaging in sports, women do attend sporting events as spectators and as exhorters of the participants. In the Sahel region, one of the most popular traditional sports, which has now been replaced by football (soccer), is wrestling. The successful wrestler is an avatar of the warrior who succeeds in defending his society against invaders.

The two songs below from Senegal reveal that women are intensely involved in supporting their particular wrestler, as they encourage their man to overcome his opponent. The second song, however, poses a pointed challenge to men who fail to win in the arena. These songs offer further evidence of women's action in the public sphere. Although the songs could have been placed in the diverse category of "praise," they constitute a distinct genre because the goal here is to have an immediate impact on the contest.

In "Yande the Wrestler," a Wolof song recorded by Luciana Penna-Diaw in the village of Ndofane in the Saloum region of Senegal, the women support the wrestler with encouraging predictions that he will win. The reference to the dress of the wrestlers refers not simply to the minimal clothing they wear but, more important, to the *gris-gris,* or talismans, with which they adorn their bodies. These small leather packets are attached by a strip of rawhide to the arm or the waist and often contain verses from the Koran on a folded piece of paper. More than decoration, they are seen as a source of protection against the power of the opponent. The repetition of the lyrics reflects the tendency to continue one's support throughout the match until one of the combatants wins.

Singer:
Yande the wrestler, wrestler, you are the one who will win. Yande the
    wrestler, you will win.

Chorus:
Yande the wrestler, wrestler, you are the one who will win. Yande the
    wrestler, wrestler, you will win.
Yande the wrestler, wrestler, you are the one who will win. Yande the
    wrestler, wrestler, you will win.
Yande the wrestler, wrestler, you are the one who will win. Yande the
    wrestler, wrestler, you will win.
Yande the wrestler, wrestler, you are the one who will win. Yande the
    wrestler, wrestler, you will win.

Singer:
Our wrestler is dressed for combat, Yande the wrestler you will win.

Chorus:
Our wrestler is dressed for combat, Yande the wrestler you will win.
Yande the wrestler you will win.
Yande the wrestler you will win.

Singer:
Our wrestler is dressed for combat, Yande the wrestler you will win.

The goal in songs of this type is to exhort and give courage to the wrestlers. But in the following song, as George Joseph points out, the women reinforce their support with a threat to the manhood of the combatants. If the men don't wrestle well, the women will step into the arena. This Wolof song was sung by Codou Mbengue from Rufisque, a city about fifteen miles southeast of Dakar. The reference to "Manjacque" is to an opponent from the Manjack people, who come from Guinea-Bissau and also live in southern Senegal and the Gambia. The song reflects what often seems to be a widespread sense of superiority over peoples to the south, including the Manjack. Manjack wrestlers, the singers appear to be saying, are not worthy opponents, and the women, if they take over, will not bother to wrestle with these men. The references both to the Manjacque and the oil falling (the oil is used by wrestlers to make their bodies more slippery) are to the defeat of the opponent.

Wrestle Men

1. Singer:
Wrestle men
Wrestle people
When there will not be men in the arena
It will be for the women.

2. Chorus:
Wrestle men
Wrestle people
When there will not be men in the arena
It will be for the women.

3. Singer:
Wrestle men
Wrestle people
When there will not be men in the arena
It will be for the women.

4. Chorus:
Wrestle men
Wrestle people
When there will not be men in the arena
It will be for the women.

5. Singer:
The Manjacque fell on the bridge
The oil fell over
I refuse to struggle with a Manjacque aayee
When there are no men in the arena
It will be for the women.

6. Chorus:
Wrestle men
Wrestle people
When there will not be men in the arena
It will be for the women.

7. Singer:
The Manjacque fell on the bridge
The oil fell over
I refuse to struggle with a Manjacque aayee
When there are no men in the arena
It will be for the women.

8. Chorus:
Wrestle men
Wrestle people
When there will not be men in the arena
It will be for the women.

9. Singer:
The Manjacque fell on the bridge
The oil fell over
I refuse to struggle with a Manjacque aayee
When there are no men in the arena
It will be for the women.

10. Chorus:
Wrestle men
Wrestle people

When there will not be men in the arena
It will be for the women.

11. Singer:
Wrestle men
Wrestle people
When there will not be men in the arena
It will be for the women.

12. Chorus:
Wrestle men
Wrestle people
When there will not be men in the arena
It will be for the women.

13. Singer:
The Manjacque fell on the bridge
The oil fell over
I refuse to struggle with a Manjacque aayee
When there are no men in the arena
It will be for the women.

PRAISE AND CRITICISM

Although praise singing is often associated with professional performers such as griottes, praise is in many ways the genre most widely performed by women in the Sahel. (In many of the songs above, there have been elements of praise, and some of them could have been placed here.) From Senegal to Niger, one finds women expressing themselves in particular genres of praise—for example, the *taasu* by various peoples in Senegal, including the Wolof and the Lebu; the *jamu* and *jammude* by the Bamana and Fulbe peoples in Mali and elsewhere; the *yabo* by the Hausa; and the *zamu* in the Songhoy-Zarma region of western Niger. In spite of local differences one finds a variety of common features. Both *zamu* and *taasu* may "glorify, praise, and mock women" (Sidikou 2001:83), often in an indirect manner that may be rather opaque to outsiders. The subjects of the songs include relatives, friends, lovers, communities, and even organizations. Professional singers who praise individuals often do so in the expectation of rewards. One can find many examples of this genre of praise song.

Muurling (2003) explains that the following Bamana song was performed by a *jelimuso*, or griotte, Sanungwe Kouyate, in Hamdallaye near Bamako, Mali, on September 5, 1999, during the marriage ceremony of Alysa Keita, the youngest daughter of the performer's patron. The song was dedicated to one of the mothers of the bride, and illustrates what Muurling sees as a tendency to emphasize differences in society, including differences between those who merit—and can pay for—praise, and those who cannot. This is hardly new: griots and griottes have been praising those of high rank, courage, and achievement for centuries. But gaining rewards for praise gives these professionals a bad reputation in the eyes of many people in their society. It has also led to the creation of a variety of words with negative connotations, including *griottage,* or empty praise to obtain money.

> Ah! When they get the crowd out
> The one who has the griot and the one who does not
> Are not the same.
> When they get the crowd out
> The one who has people and the one who doesn't have any
> Are not the same.
> Iyw! Awa, that is done because of hope,
> Good mother.

Janson (2003) recorded a similar song in Mansajang Kunda, the Gambia. Jeneba Kuyateh is begging for money from her patron. But although it may appear that the begging singer stands at the bottom of the social ladder, in fact she is, as Janson points out, exercising a form of control over her patron when she warns, "If you refuse to give to a griot / God would not give to you either." The expression *turuti marati* is onomatopoeia that Janson translates approximately as "going up and down."

> Give to the griot
> My patron, give to me
> Oh, give to the griot
> My patron, give to me
> Give to the griot
> My patron, give to me
> *Foro musu jawoolu turuti marati* [The way a bad woman walks]
> Those whose griot
> would never get a hundred [*dalasi,* about US$10]
> Give to the griot
> My patron, give to me
> If you refuse to give to a griot,
> God would not give to you either
> Give to the griot

My patron, give to me
If you give to a griot,
God will give you something
Give to the griot
My patron, give to me
I say give to the griot
European, give to me

Give to the griot
My patron, give to me
Foro musu jawoolu turuti marati
Those whose griot—
Give to the griot
My patron, give to me
If you refuse to give to a griot,
God would not give to you either
Give to the griot
God will give you something
Give to the griot
My patron, give to me
If you refuse to give to a griot,
God would not give to you either

Give to the griot
My patron, give to me
Foro musu jawoolu turuti marati
Those whose griot
would never get a hundred [*dalasi*]
Give to the griot
My patron, give to me
I say give to the griot
My patron, give to me.

The search for rewards for praise singing is often not simply a one-way request, but involves a complex relationship in which the status of the donor depends on the recognition by the singer of his or her status. In other words, a ruler or noble cannot hold this high status unless someone recognizes him or her as having earned it by rewarding griots.

In the Songhoy song below, recorded by Hale on February 18, 1989 in Yatakala, Niger, the singers Pouré Atta and Gitu Sagado emphasize that there is an indissoluble link between a ruler and a *jesere weyboro,* a female griot. In the body of the song, the performers seek rewards from the chief, but at the end of their wishes expand to the entire town. Everyone has great expectations of the leader. With the metaphor of the eyes, the singers insist that a chief has to lead not only with rewards for his *jeserey,* but also by manifesting his vision for society—in this case, the residents of the community. This song was addressed to the canton chief in Yatakala, who was listening from a window in his house, close to the singers. *Sunfuleyni* is a term of praise and respect for the chief. The translation below is by Aissata Niandou.

> Father and mother of the poor people,
> Husband of beautiful ladies
> When you are away the town is not interesting
> When you are away the people are not happy.
> Husband of beautiful ladies,
> Greetings to the noble Maiga [descendants of Askia Mohammed].
> When you are away the town is not interesting
> When you are away the people are not happy.
> Be our mother,
> Be our father,
> Provide us with clothing
> *Sunfuleyni*
> Be the salt we use with our gravy
> Be the oil we need for our porridge
> Provide us with caftans and trousers
> Then we will be proud.
> The prince who comes to feed us will make us proud,
> The prince who comes to provide us with clothing,
> The prince who comes to provide us with food
> The prince who comes to provide us with shoes,
> You are our eyes,
> you are our mirror,
> you are our hands and feet
> And legs that we use to walk.

This notion of interdependency appears also in a Bamana song by the well-known singer Ami Koita, which Dorothea Schulz published in 2001. She explains that "*jeliw* [griots] offer face-saving services to the patron, asserting that the patron depends on his *jeli* for the management of his reputation. At the same time, *jeliw* will subtly remind their patrons that clients can always become disloyal if their patrons are too 'greedy'" (148). In the following excerpt, Ami Koita cautions her patron Tata Sira.

The people who give support [the *jigi*] to others are not many
People of confidence are not many
You should love the person, Tata Sira,
Who is interested in you
You should separate yourself from the person
Who is not interested in you. . . .
If you become a help for the *jeliw,* Tata Doukouré [another name for Tata Sira],
The *jeliw* of Manding will speak of you at many places. . . .
I love those people who love me
I separate from those people who are not interested in me.

Hunters are also the subject of praise, and there is an entire category of songs about them. Hunters have a powerful reputation because of their ability to track, kill, and bring home animals whose flesh keeps people alive. Unlike agriculture, hunting is to a great extent an individual activity. Hunters may go out in small groups, but it is often an individual arrow, spear, or shot that stops an animal, with the weapons of other members of the group finishing the job. The following Maninka song was recorded by Jan Jansen in March 1989 from one of the most famous professional female singers in Mali, the *jelimuso* Siramori Diabaté, at her home in Kela. It was translated by Brahima Camara and Jansen.

The singer compounds her praise of hunters by associating them with political heroes of the past, notably Sundiata, the founder of the Mali empire, and Tiramaghan Traoré, one of his generals who challenged him. Readers familiar with this epic in one of its many translations will find a variety of Mande themes embedded in the song. But like many West African epics, this song is extremely complex, and not fully accessible even to native speakers of the language; the translations of two of the lines are indicated in brackets as temporary. In the lyrics below, the singer gives two different terms for antelopes, one specific (Buffon), the other more general (Koba).

This melody is dedicated to the hunter heroes
Aaa, the hunter hero hasn't arrived
The cat that passes one single time
Has sown terror at sunrise
Long time ago
This melody was dedicated to the hunter heroes
Aaa, the hunter hero hasn't arrived
The owl from the mountain of Kanjan hasn't arrived
I'll tell you the person who slays and pushes the wild animals is feared
Long time ago
Not all people know how to dance to the melody of the *janjo*

The hunter hero from the mountain of Kanjan isn't there
Jankina, the hunter hero, isn't afraid
The owls have brought antelope horns
The owls have brought them
The owls have brought horns of Buffon's antelopes
The owls have brought them
The owls have brought horns of Koba antelopes
Really, he isn't afraid, Jankina, the hunter hero
Aaa, aaa, aaa, the bird of the days of the past
Peace and hail to you
Be patient, followers of Mohammed
Isn't it that some people sleep
While others are awake
You compare the brave
Well, there is a big difference among the brave
Isn't it, eh, eh, eh, life!
Are there many hunter heroes in one's life?
The hunter heroes have become scarce
Aaa, to which hunter hero do I refer?
Owl—for you the wilderness
Kunkunba and Bantanba
Nyani-nyani and Kanbasiga
Kayirumajikiso
Namitè, Namijokola
Isn't it true that some [who are] brave are more courageous than others
Aaa, you are a hunter hero
Bebe Jigi is a hunter who loves the bow
Aaa, really numerous are the hunter heroes
Traveling salesmen who walk the entire night, hail to your efforts
Traveling salesmen who walk the entire day, hail to your numerous efforts
Do you know to which hunter hero I refer?
Hunter heroes of the waters, hail too, to your efforts
Jèbè is the small tip of the pirogue
Jèbè is the large tip of the pirogue
Jèbè is the small tip of the first *juba*
Jèbè is the large tip of the huge *juba*
Children of the Somono women, where are you, hunter heroes?
Look at Muntaka Kamara!
Fasinè Sokore, Alama Sokore, Kasumu Sokore
Aaa, aaa, I recall the hunter hero

Eee, eee, the owl-son of Bintu
Is there in the bush far away
Naman really is a hunter hero who loves the bow
Spouses of Somono women, where did the *kolon* spend the night?
Spouses of Somono women, where did the *kolon* spend the night?
Aaa, owl-son of Bintu, where did the *kolon* spend the night?
Owl-son of Bintu, where did the Nile perches spend the night?
Aaa, the great traveling salesman . . . Allah
Isn't it so that
Naren Makan Jata in his identity as Sirifila Makan Konatè has arrived
He who glances through the big and the small brushwood
Apologize to me
Really, brave men have become scarce
It is really difficult to know Mande
Mande is here
The turning well
The well you talk about
Which some people call "the turning well"
In that well won't drop a blind person
But only the few people from Mande who can see
Certain people know Sunsun, but don't know Manko
Certain people know Manko, but don't know Sunsun
Aaa, powerful traveling salesmen, the hunter hero hasn't gone to sleep
One day, Sirifila Makan Konatè convoked the brave
Rise up, rise up, please, braves of Mande
That each of you will demonstrate his capacities
That after this day this country, Mande, won't be without real men
This being said, Konè from Kasawura, Konè, drinker of large quantities of
     water
Sirifila Makan Konatè descends from the Konè
This being said, the ancestor of the Kamara
Wana Faran Kamara from Sibi
Wana Faran Kamara from Tabun
Wana Faran Kamara from Nyènkèma
If you cut his arm in the morning
Watch how it recovers
An arrow killed Kaman the Tall
And sorcerers gave Kaman the final blow
As a hunter like lightning
Kaman the Tall drew his sword from the sheath that hangs on his hips

And transfixed the Mande hill, thus creating the arch of entrance and exit
    of Kaman the Tall
That is the way the griots tell it
Where have Tiramagan and Kankejan gone!
He said: "Rise up! Brave men of Mande, if you don't rise up, the buffalo will
    soon exterminate Mande
Every day it makes three victims
Brave men of Mande, rise up!"
Fakòli, the son of Koman Kòdòma, the killer of enemies, rose up
Fakòli with the big head, Fakòli with the big mouth
Kòli with the big umbilical, Kòli without umbilical
He marched, marched, and marched
Oh! It is not easy to see the buffalo
Yes, powerful traveling salesman, it is difficult to see the buffalo of Mande
Who was also called to appear?
Soma Dòbi, the ancestor of the Konatè
The horn of an antelope kills someone, that object will kill its owner in
    Mande [tentative translation]
The horn of a duiker kills someone, that object will kill its owner in Mande
Sirifila Makan Konatè said uh, uh
It really isn't easy to see this buffalo
Sirifila Makan Konatè ordered to call Tiramagan
The servant who digs his own tomb as well as his master's
The black dog without horns, the son of Nakana
If you don't rise up, Tiramagan
The buffalo will soon exterminate Mande
It makes three victims a day
Tiramagan and Kankejan rose up
He went to see Siriman Kanda Ture
Manjan Berete from Tonbondò
"Siriman Kanda Ture, do help me
Tonbondò Manjan Berete, you must help me to beat this buffalo
Because many brave men from Mande have left to chase it in vain"
The first and last Koranic scholar of Mande
He did a magic spell on the wings of a partridge that he sent to fly away
Then he said to Tiramagan, "Rise up, you will beat the buffalo
Searching for the buffalo, you will meet
Two old ladies collecting wood—don't you ever pass them, Tiramagan"
Tiramagan, the king of behind-the-river, took his quiver and his bow

And said that he would go after the buffalo
Arriving at the crossroads, the crossing of the roads,
He saw two old ladies gathering wood
"Hello, grandmothers" he yelled
"Why do you greet us, Tiramagan, we don't work for you"
"I greet you, because you are comparable to my mother"
He went into the bush and collected two piles of wood
That he deposited on the crossroads, the crossing of the roads
"Grandmothers, come and take this wood
And return to your house, because you are tired
You suffer under the sun"
Tiramagan, you have become . . .
You are a little, provoking child
Tiramagan, you have become . . .
You are a bellicose man
You are in search of the buffalo
That makes three victims every day
Tiramagan, I am this buffalo, it is not easy to see me
Tiramagan, what you want
I will give myself to you, servant who digs his own tomb as well as his
    master's
You, dog-without-horns, son of Nakana
I will give myself to you, and it will be remembered in your praise song
    from here to the afterlife
If you look for the buffalo, go and look in the big woods at the lake
When you see the buffalo, one eye is golden
When you see the buffalo, one eye is silver
Tiramagan, when you see the buffalo, if you don't fear
You, servant who digs his own tomb as well as his master's
If you beat the buffalo, it will be remembered in my praise song from here
    to the afterlife
Tiramagan and Kankejan, king of behind-the-river, I will give myself to you
Tiramagan took his quiver and bow and started to march
He saw the buffalo
Which had one eye golden
He saw the buffalo
Which had one eye silver
He bent, like a reaping hook, a reaping hook to cut the *nèrè* tree in Mande
He mustered his strength in such a way . . .

And his hand produced evil, the celestial drum
Tiramagan beat the buffalo
Tukuru and Kasinè, Kasinè and Kasinèsa
Sèlèn Fabore, Danka Fabure
Makanta the Black and Makanta the White
Dog-without-horns, son of Nakana
You beat the buffalo to make this part of your praise song, you, king of
    behind-the-river
Tiramagan beat the buffalo and the griots of Mande say
That Tiramagan and Kankejan should be glorified
That the quiver and the bow will be given to Tiramagan
Tiramagan, he is the servant who digs his own tomb
Aaa, the lance may refuse, but Tiramagan doesn't fear
Tiramagan, the servant who digs his own tomb
To Tiramagan has been given the call for war
Tiramagan, the servant who digs his own tomb
Hail to your efforts, hail to your efforts, Tiramagan and Kankejan
Hail to your efforts, hail to your efforts, Muke Musa and Muke Dantuman,
    hail to your efforts
Aaa, Tiramagan and Kankejan didn't fear
The slave who digs his own tomb as well as his master's
This melody has been dedicated to Tiramagan and Kankejan
Soriyo, aaa, dimè
The horse isn't insidious, but the reins are insidious
The horse isn't insidious, but the . . . is insidious
The servant who digs his own tomb as well as his master's
Do . . . show the gunpowder publicly, so Tiramagan will come out
Tiramagan, the servant who digs his own tomb
Aaa, the lance may refuse, but Tiramagan isn't afraid
Tiramagan, the slave who digs his own tomb.

Professional singers often praise themselves, either indirectly by listing their
ancestors, as did the *jeli* Mamadou Kouyaté, who narrated much of the version of *Sundiata* recorded by Djibril Tamsir Niane, or more openly, as in the
improvised song below by a Moor *iggiw,* Yakuta mint Ali Warakan, which was
recorded by H. T. Norris (1968:53). In the case of Mamadou Kouyaté, his self-
praise served to emphasize the value of the epic he was about to recount. In the
example below, the singer may have composed the song in order to persuade
the researcher of her importance. In the song, *huri* refers to virgins in paradise,
who will be the rewards for men who arrive there.

From what ruby, O Lord of the throne, is Yākūta?
From the source of the pearl and ruby she is fashioned.
In the form of a dark-eyed *huri* he has shaped her,
As he wished, and the people love Yākūta.
Yākūta, her renown is supreme, and any youth
Who says the name Yākūta, then her name is his sustenance.
There is no lady like her in Mauritania
Nor in Senegal, nor Gambia, nor Futa [a geographic region].
She is the full moon, but without a blemish in it, and
Her spouse is the sea, but without great fish in it.

In the Islamic societies of West Africa, the professional singer used to be in some ways a rival with the religious leader—for example, the *marabout* or the imam—for the attention of the people (Hale 1990: 45–46). Today, these performers remind listeners that they, too, are practicing Muslims, and that their profession is rooted in Islam, which is evidenced by some of the origin tales told about the griots (Hale 1998:64–67). One also finds frequent references in their praises to the blessings that will flow to the donor from the griots and griottes. Janson (2003) recorded the following song about *jaliyaa*, the profession of Mande griots and griottes. The sense of the song is that these singers are as Muslim as anyone else because God created their profession, just as he created kingship. Both are part of the same world, and both deserve the same respect.

Yeah, *jaliyaa,* God has created *jaliyaa*
Yeah, *jaliyaa,* God has created *jaliyaa*
He also created kingship
There is mercy in *jaliyaa*
There is fame in *jaliyaa*

God has created *jaliyaa*
Talking of *jaliyaa*
Always *jaliyaa*
Okay, *jaliyaa* does not take place every day
Good evening with *jaliyaa*
Griottes and griots
Singers and master singers
Are all honored in *jaliyaa*
Bards. . . .

Yeah, *jaliyaa,* God has created *jaliyaa*
God is the one who created *jaliyaa*
And he is the one who created kingship.

Depending on the local tradition, a song may be sung to celebrate the memory of someone who has died. Diawara (1990:135) published this excerpt from a well-known Soninké song titled "Silaami," which is sung only for old men who have served a ruler or for young men who have a reputation for valor and generosity. Diawara explains that the singers seek to convey their own beauty and dignity by comparing themselves with precious metals.

The gold is crying [for the death of the hero]!
The silver cries!
The stalwart ones who deserve to have Silaami dedicated to them
Are no longer here—they no longer exist!
Those who seek a name and fame are done!
In the old days (let's just say it)
They didn't sing Silaami except for celebrations
Then they sang it in the countryside
But in the distant countryside.

APPROPRIATE BEHAVIOR AND ATTITUDES

Another concern of women is the appropriate behavior of other women. Lisa McNee explains that in a song performed during a naming ceremony, or *ngente* in Wolof, in Louga, Senegal, on May 26, 1993 (2000:34–35), the singers criticize a woman who is unwilling to share food with her sisters-in-law. They make their views known in an indirect fashion by expressing the hope that the baby will someday marry a good woman rather than a bad woman. The goal is to suggest subtly to the child's mother to change her ways by implying that she is a bad woman. The words in brackets are those of McNee. The use of J. rather than the full name is designed to protect the identity of the subject.

Faatu J. [name of the child's mother]
The woman who clears [tidies] her house
So that her family [has room to] live there
Pleases me more
Than she who clears her house of her family [so that the family moves out]
Faatu J.
The woman who clears her house of her family [so that her family moves out]
Faatu J.
The woman who clears her house
To make room for her family
That one is worth an Arab horse
She's worth a stallion

And deserves a car
But a woman who clears her house
So that the family leaves—
That one deserves to be beaten to death.

Oh, may you have a wife who brings you luck
With the woman who suits your destiny
Whatever you attempt will succeed
May your wife improve your fate
If your wife brings no luck
Whatever you build will fall.
May your wife bring you luck.

In other cases, praise is directed without nuance at a woman who has done good things for her people. This song, recorded by Kate Modic on June 2, 1991 (1996:163), was performed at a *denkundi,* or naming ceremony, and includes both the singer and a chorus.

MARIAM: O Fanta you fill the hope!
    A person can't be strong unless your hope is strong.
CHORUS: O Fanta you fill the hope!
    A person can't be strong unless your hope is strong.
MARIAM: I say that one day, Fanta, you filled the hope
    The close relative road, you filled the hope in me
    The lover of the birthchild, you filled the hope for me
    Honest person, you filled the hope in me
    Being correct with your neighbors, you filled the hope, Fanta
    In the wedding of the birthchild, you filled my hope
    The hope of the entrance room of Daoudabougou isn't filled early
    The comforter of the hungry people, you filled my hope.

A similar form of praise for a woman was narrated by Oumougna de Dantchandou in Zarma, Niger; recorded by Fatima Mounkaïla; and translated by Mounkaïla and Diouldé Laya (2003).

Hamsatou, the mother of Maygounia
Wife of the father of Dalaîzé
Receive my congratulations, Hamsatou
The wishes of your adversaries will have no hold on you.
Because, when one considers the innate luck that you have been able to grasp
No adversary even had its eyes open
To be able to push and catch it.

Hamsatou, the mother of Hammadou,
Mother of Hassan and mother of Maygounia
The ridge beam of the neighborhood on the side of the hill
It is while waiting for a day like this one
That a Zarma daughter ought to eat her millet chaff
So that her throat saves her from shame
It is my courage that has saved me from misfortune
Flower of a calabash of the master of the Sudan
The white administrator cannot throw me in prison
As for the qadi, who is a man of justice
His just verdicts cannot wrong me
And the village exciser cannot complain to me.

Hamsatou, the native of Tchôta
Who knows how to say sweet and agreeable words
Who offers words worthy of princely beings
She told me: "Dagni, the mother of Oummou
This activity of hairdresser that you do,
Avoid doing it for an ill-loved wife"
For an ill-loved wife will devalue my coiffure
"Stingy people should stop
Thinking of getting closer to you, mother of Oummou."

In contrast with praising model behavior, other songs focus on those who do the reverse, who denigrate people. Bah Diakité (2003) recorded this Bamana song from southern Mali in which the narrator condemns those who criticize others. Although the singer expresses the message of the song in rather direct terms, she also frames her warning in sayings and metaphors, some of which may be fully understandable only to those steeped in the language and culture of the society. Nevertheless, in the final metaphor about vermin, there is no doubt about what should happen to those who attempt to diminish the reputations of others.

The detractors are mistaken
Whoever has the talent will know how to deal with them
The detractors are mistaken
Whoever has some goodness is rich.
Slander can do nothing against the taste of honey
Slander cannot take away the whiteness of milk
The detractors are mistaken
The songs of those who possess are rich

The detractors are mistaken
Whoever has the talent will know how to deal with them
The razor errs
The whiskers regrow
The ax is in the lure
Will regrow
The chicken is wrong to boast
The threshing ground cannot be without grain
But when the bird hatches
Then the locust stops parading
Shame to detractors!
They are merely vermin
That one must crush with one's foot.

In another poem recorded by Diakité (2003), the singer and the chorus exhort women to have patience in dealing with the challenges of life, such as difficult mothers-in-law, the loss of children, and widowhood.

The singer:
1. Patience, everything comes out of patience
2. Yes, everything depends on patience
   Chorus:
3. Patience, everything depends on patience
4. You, women, I say everything depends on patience
   The singer:
5. You, women, everything depends on patience
6. We're down here to talk
7. Let everybody be patient
8. Women's widowhood is harmful
9. Let's be patient
10. Women's loss of children is harmful [has no good aspect]
11. Let everybody be patient
12. I tell you that loss of brothers and sisters [is harmful, has no good aspect]
13. Let's be patient
14. To each individual her destiny
15. Not all mothers-in-law are grateful
16. Lose not patience, dear girl
    Chorus:
17. Patience, everything depends on patience
18. You, women, I say everything depends on patience.

BEAUTY

Personal beauty is a concern for most women for a variety of reasons: to be attractive to men, to compete with other women, to boost their self-esteem, and to take part in a cooperative activity which becomes something of a social event.

One of the most widespread ways of increasing one's beauty is tattooing, which in West Africa is done with locally made ink or powder and long, thin thorns from acacia, breadfruit, and other trees or with steel needles. It may involve one woman who does the tattooing, others who assist, and others who sing to help the individual being tattooed deal with the pain of the numerous thorn pricks. This process requires both patience and the ability to withstand pain for several hours as the tattooer works to create fine patterns around the lips and on other parts of the subject's face.

In this song, recorded by George Joseph (2003), the singer emphasizes the large number of thorns gathered for her and reminds listeners of the amount of pain she will need to endure. She adds that someone of her birth will be able to handle the pain, and reproaches those who think they can discern a reaction to the process. In other words, nothing will cause her to deviate from her goal of obtaining the tattoos without uttering a complaint. Her reaction conveys a form of courage.

> It is for me that they have gathered thorns
> It is for me that they gathered breadfruit thorns
> It is for me that they gathered acacia thorns.
> An entire *moud* [a measure of weight] of tattooing powder
> An entire basket of thorns
> This cannot end the life of a well-born girl
> I refuse shame, I refuse reproach.
> Daughter of so-and-so and so-and-so
> I refuse shame, I refuse reproach
> O, so-and-so or so-and-so, I refuse shame, I refuse reproach.

Another sign of beauty in many Sahelian cultures is fatness. For example, Sidikou describes the *maani foori,* which is "a tradition originally related to the cycles of farming and cultivation. . . . It is a complex and extensive ritual about women honoring their bodies through food, songs, and dance steps" (2001:59). Men are not allowed to attend *maani foori* ceremonies. She adds that thin women are looked down upon in a relationship that is marked by the power of one group of women over another, which creates a "shadow structure" in a society that, for the most part, does not allow them to "share power with men" (63). In the following song (72), a thin woman vows to become fat. *Dara* is a dance step, and *songolol* is onomatopoeia for a tall woman who is all skin and bones. The phrase "I will reach this" is accompanied by an opening of the hands.

Fat is gold
It is beautiful on everyone's chest
I have *dara*'s back
I have *dara*'s chest
Once I'm fat,
With my father's blessings I will reach this
Dara should be *daramu*
The *songolol* one will not dance *dara*.

HEALTH

Although the general health of people in the Sahel has improved with greater access to services and sustained efforts to eliminate some diseases, efforts that in many cases are leading to a demographic shift of fewer births (since more of the children survive), threats such as AIDS still present great challenges to communities. These concerns are now addressed in songs. In some areas, a new genre has appeared—what has been called *development songs*—that, as in the lyrics below, urges people to adopt practices to protect themselves from disease. Louise Bourgault assembled a diverse selection of these songs, performed by women and men, professional and nonprofessional singers, for her book *Playing for Life: Performance in Africa in the Age of AIDS* (2003).

In the song below by Dene Issebere, produced in cassette form and distributed by the Center for Development and Population Activities and Population Services International in Bamako, Mali, in 2002, the emphasis is on the need for men to use condoms. The singer uses one of many French terms for condom, *capote*, which is short for *capote anglaise*.

Make it your companion
These days, let's make the condom our companion

At this time, let's make the condom our friend
Dangerous diseases are numerous, make the condom a friend
Make it a companion, make it a friend
Make it a companion, make it a friend
Make it a companion, make it a friend.

There are treatments for some diseases
There are no treatments for other diseases

What's needed is protection
Nothing is of greater value than protection
Make it a companion
In these times, let's make the condom our companion.

These days, make the condom our friend
There are too many dangerous diseases—AIDS
My dear friends, there are too many sexual diseases of which AIDS is the
     most dangerous.
If you catch it, it is incurable
The only way to protect ourselves against AIDS is the use of the *capote*
As a means of protecting against these dangerous
Diseases is the use of a *capote*
My brothers and sisters protect yourself. The *capote* is not your enemy.
It is instead your friend
Make it your companion
In these times, let's make the condom our companion
Make it your companion, make the *capote* your friend.

BELIEF AND RITUAL

One descriptor for belief, whether it is in the tenets of Christianity, Islam, or a
more localized system rooted in a particular culture, is, in the words of historian Bogumil Jewsiewicki, "social fact, not a false consciousness" (1987:20; cited
in Hale 1998:23). Belief influences people not only in how they view the world,
but also in their behavior, especially in rituals, which may include a wide range
of ceremonies, for example initiating the individual into a different status in
society, or seeking possession by a spirit. Women may participate in various
rituals with their songs.

In this short Serer song, whose lyrics are endlessly repeated, a woman responds to a man who questions her belief. Charles Katy (2003b) explains that
the woman is on her way to the sanctuary of the village of Yaayeem to conduct rituals on behalf of the community. En route she encouters a man named
Ngode Baas who wants to know where she is going with all of her religious
paraphernalia. *Jogma* is a short form of Jogomaay, the spirit of the sanctuary
for the village.

Ngode Baas you are seeing me bearing something
Man you dare ask me
Where am I going?
I am going to praise Jogma Yaayeem.

Katy also offers a Serer song that relates to the family and its connections to the ancestors. He explains that an individual offers prayers to his or her ancestors in the hope that happiness will result. The altar on which the libation is poured links the past, present, and future of the family.

> Jombo Xaane, my ancestor
> It is time to do my libation
> Ngoor Ndebaan, my ancestor
> Benediction gives prosperity like Maliyam's one.

At the other end of the Sahel, in Niger, the Hausa and other peoples, such as the Songhoy-Zarma, maintain a tradition of possession ceremonies known as *bori*. Participants become possessed as they connect with the many spirits linked to the *bori* cult. Boubé Namaiwa (2003) contributed this song by Taguimba Bouzou, an internationally known singer from the Azna people in the Arewa area, part of the Hausa-speaking world of Niger and Nigeria, who devoted much of her career to singing at *bori* ceremonies. Many of her songs were dedicated to some of the two hundred spirits who are part of the pantheon of the *bori* cult, but she did not cause people to go into a state of possession with her songs. Rather, she provided the context for both the participants and the audience.

In the following song one hears the names of many people, spirits, and places that are part of the *bori* network. But only those who are familiar with the *bori* beliefs can decipher the importance and the roles of these spirits. Namaiwa has added some clarifications in brackets. The reference to a *violinist* is to the player of a one-stringed instrument called a *godje* that adherents of the *bori* often use to open the path to the spirits.

> In the past our heads were completely black in a pot [they were ignorant].
> Clean your ears,
> Bellah is a fire player.
> Clean your ears,
> Bellah plays with fire.
> *Bori* is spectacular,
> *Bori* is joyful,
> Make ourselves human,
> Where is the healer?
> I thank the healer,
> Porridge of millet with milk,
> Paste of millet with meat,
> Where do I go now?

I'll go to Fadama,
Arkiawo is waiting for me.
Kassu: Arkiawo who has roasted meat. We must go to Gobro!
Where are the youth of this ceremony?
Where are the youth of this ceremony?
Where are the young *bori* devotees?
Make ourselves humans,
It never takes life,
Where am I going now?
I'm going to Birni.
Abu is waiting for me
Tadebe is waiting for me
Dango is waiting for me.
I thank Tani,
I thank Tashi,
I thank Ba'ou,
Madugu Dan Koale,
Abu is waiting for me.
Bellah the great destroyer.
Kassu: Those who insult you have pity on their heads, *Barmu dan guzaye
    Jikan nana.*
May Allah bring us the healer. Allah protect us from diseases!
Where am I going now?
Where am I going now?
Where am I going now?
I'm going to Kore.
There is the healer Gagno,
Kumunde is waiting for me,
Our husband with Ady,
I thank Igge.
Where am I going now?
I'm going to Kiada,
Allami is waiting for me,
Tabizo is waiting for me,
Sane is waiting for me,
Tarwa is waiting for me,
Dawda is waiting for me.
I greet Bawanke,
And I greet him again,
Clean your ears,

I greet this crowd,
I greet this crowd,
Those of Bellah, the great destroyer.
Kassu: Dan Bina is in Kiada. There is Dan Bina in Kiada.
One day, only news will remain. *Bori* can't prevent death. Those who drank
their water will go.
Wait a minute, spectator,
Wait a minute, spectator,
Wait a minute, violinist,
Wait a minute, violinist.
Bellah is the lover of Dango,
Bellah never accepts advice.
I'm going to Beshemi,
Jikko is waiting for me,
Hure is waiting for me.
Where are the youth of the ceremony?
May Allah accept more than me!
Where are the youth of the ceremony?
I'm here to greet you,
Devotees of Bellah the destroyer,
Bellah player with fire,
Call me the mad one.

4 —⟳ *Death*

Songs about death help listeners to come to grips with the inevitability of the end of life, and also remind them of the fragility of existence. Underlying the subject is awareness of the need to live in a manner that respects the larger world of the living and the dead. In the songs below, the singers express concern about the consequences of death for themselves and for their audiences.

UBIQUITY AND ACCEPTANCE OF DEATH

In the following Bamana song, recorded by Bah Diakité (2003) in southern Mali, the singers warn that death occurs everywhere, and that one must be ready to accept it.

The singer:
1. If you look for a village where nobody dies
2. You won't see that village
   Chorus:
3. If you look for a village where nobody dies
4. You won't see that village
   The singer:
5. If you look for a village where nobody dies
6. You won't see such a village, daughter
7. If ever you look for a village
8. Where eminent persons don't die, my dear Ayadian
9. You'll never see that village
10. If ever you look for a village
11. Where children don't die,
12. You won't see that village
13. If you look at a village
14. Where death doesn't make widows, Ayadian
15. I don't know where such a village might be.
16. If you look for a village

17. Where one loses not his dear child, Ayadian
18. You'll never find that village
19. If you look for a village where nobody dies
20. You'll never find that village.

CRUELTY OF DEATH

Diakité (2003) also recorded a song about the pain of losing a good person who, the singer implies, does not merit death at this point in his life.

The singer:
1. If ever death spares someone
2. For positive deeds, it would have spared Ladji
   Chorus:
3. If ever death spares someone
4. For positive deeds in Bambara land it would have spared Ladji
   The singer:
5. But death won't spare anybody for his positive deeds
6. If ever death spared someone
7. The man who sowed hope among fatherless children that was Titian,
8. Ladji Titian would have been spared
9. But death won't spare anyone
10. The man who sowed hope among starving people that was Titian,
11. It would have spared Ladji Titian
12. The man who sowed hope among brotherless and sisterless, Ladji
13. Death would have spared Ladji in this world
14. If ever death spared someone
15. The man who sowed hope among widows that was Ladji Titian
16. Death would have spared Titian
17. If ever death spared someone
18. The man who sowed hope among Muslims that was Titian
19. Death would have spared Titian in this world
20. If ever death spared someone
21. The man who sowed hope among hopeless that was Titian
22. Death shouldn't have taken Titian.

FEAR ABOUT THE CARE OF CHILDREN

Songs about death convey many emotions, but perhaps the most poignant is a mother's fear about what will happen to her children after her death. In the Jula song below, recorded by Jean Derive (1986:360), a duo and a chorus express the hope that after the woman's death a co-wife will assume responsibility for the child's care. Derive has added the word *but* in brackets to emphasize the opposition between the two sentiments conveyed here: acceptance of death, and fear for the future of a child.

Duo:
Hey! Death is not difficult for me,
[but] I am going to die and leave today a child who will suffer
Co-wife, here is my child, co-wife, here is my child
Chorus:
Death is not difficult for me,
[but] I die and leave today my child in suffering
Co-wife, here is my child, co-wife, here is my child!

SOLITUDE OF THE SURVIVOR

In this Bamana song, recorded by Pascal Couloubaly (1990) from a woman in the town of NCòla, Mali, the listener discovers the depth of loneliness caused by the death of anyone in the extended family.

Solitude is bad eh
Solitude is bad eh

The hope of a woman, it's the life of a mother
That death comes to take little by little
Solitude is bad eh

The hope of a wife, it's the life of a father
That death comes to take little by little
Solitude is bad eh

The hope of a woman, it is the life of a husband
That death comes to take little by little
Solitude is bad eh

The hope of a woman, it's the life of a child
That death comes to take little by little
Solitude is bad eh
Solitude is bad, women of NCòla the great
Solitude is bad eh

The hope of a woman, it is the life of a relative
That death comes to take little by little
Solitude is bad eh
Solitude is bad eh
Solitude is bad eh.

Appendix

ORIGINAL TRANSCRIPTIONS OF SELECTED SONGS

**Beeyoo Beeyoo
(Billy Goat; George Joseph)**

1. *Debbe*
Beeyoo, beeyoo, beeyoo bey
Man sama doom day jooy,
Aayoo bey.

2. *Awu*
Beeyoo, beeyoo, beeyoo bey
Man sama doom day jooy,
Aayoo bey.

3. *Debbe*
Beeyoo, beeyoo, beeyoo bey
Man sama doom day jooy,
Aayoo bey.

4. *Awu*
Beeyoo, beeyoo, beeyoo bey
Man sama doom day jooy,
Aayoo bey.

5. *Debbe*
Man sama doom jee
Bu ko neexee jooy
Mbaxar Biram
Beeyoo, beeyoo, beeyo bey.

6. *Awu*
Beeyoo, beeyoo, beeyoo bey
Man sama doom day jooy,
Aayoo bey.

7. *Debbe*
Taala sama nenne
Bu la neexee jooy,
Mbaxar Biram
Aayoo beyoo, beyoo, beeyoo ndaw.

8. *Awu*
Beeyoo, beeyoo, beeyoo bey
Man sama doom day jooy,
Aayoo bey.

9. *Debbe*
Maali Kumba Joor
Degan Fara Làmb
Saa Njukki caatum Joor
Yow loo di jooy
Taala sama doom jii bëgguma ci lu ko
naqari dara
Beeyoo bey.

10. *Awu*
Beeyoo, beeyoo, beeyoo bey
Man sama doom day jooy,
Aayoo bey.

11. *Debbe*
Taala Guy sama doom jee,
Yàlla ngay maam,
Mbaxar Biram
Beeyoo, beeyoo, aayoo ndaw.

12. *Awu*
Beeyoo, beeyoo, beeyoo bey

Man sama doom day jooy,
Aayoo bey.

13. *Debbe*
Yaa di sama benn
Yaa ma ba jomb ñaan
Mbaxar Biram
Beeyoo bey, yaay aayoo bey.

14. *Awu*
Beeyoo, beeyoo, beeyoo bey
Man sama doom day jooy,
Aayoo bey.

15. *Debbe*
Taala Ndongo Faal mii
Bu ko neexee reew
Ndax daa gore
Aayoo, aayoo, beeyoo bey.

16. *Awu*
Beeyoo, beeyoo, beeyoo bey
Man sama doom day jooy,
Aayoo bey.

17. *Debbe*
Taala Bañ Ngóone, Degen
Xawuma looy jooy,
Mbaxar Biram
Beeyoo, bey yaay, beeyoo ndaw.

18. *Awu*
Beeyoo, beeyoo, beeyoo bey
Man sama doom day jooy,
Aayoo bey.

19. *Debbe*
Baay Faal ma ca Koso
Bu la neexee reew
Mbaxar Biram
Beeyoo ndeysaan
Aayoo bey.

20. *Awu*
Beeyoo, beeyoo, beeyoo bey
Man sama doom day jooy,
Aayoo bey.

21. *Debbe*
Man sama doom day jooy

Ma di ko doxantoo
Beeyoo bey yaay, aayoo bey.

22. *Awu*
Beeyoo, beeyoo, beeyoo bey
Man sama doom day jooy,
Aayoo bey.

**Stop Crying Bride
(Thomas A. Hale and Aissata Niandou)**

Dangay, dangay he nyaale
Danga ya ma
Din anzuraay ka tun ka ni waw
Ma he ma dangay
Din alboray ka tun ka ni waw
Ma he ma dangay
Din kurnye nya ka tun kin waw
Ma he ma dangay.
Din kurnye nya ka tun kin waw
Ma he ma dangay.
Amma gambu sambu
Sinda haawi sakaala se.

**Now she took the calabash of millet
(Aissata Sidikou)**

935   Sohon a na haini gaaso sambu,
       A na dumi gaaso dake a ra.
       Kuhyo na kalama jase.
       I go ga fakaarey,
       I go ga fakaaray.
940   Kurhyo go bunga
       A na haini sambu,
       Ne bey gaasu no bor ga sambu,
       Ga dira ga duma nda.
       A ma duma ne dey kal a ma koy man
       Ne cine.
945   Bunga koono no a go ga daabu
       Nan kan a to,
       A ma haino gussam,
       Bunga far a a ma daabu.
       A ma ye ga koy ga kuu.
950   I foy ga duma, i foy ga duma,
       Kal almari i ka ga kani.

Suba mo biya ga bo
Wok an cindi i goy hay alula
Kul I na faro dabandi.
955 I ka, I hyumey,
I go ga gor ga fulamzam
I go ga fakaarey
Kurhyo ne a se
A ne "ni dii wargida,"
960 A ne "wallahi ni dii,
Sohon gorey te inga daa.
Hari wo nankan Irkoye na kayandi
No a ga kay."
A ne "sohon ay na nil sallama.
Ni feyyan tira ne,
965 Ma sobey ga koy."
A ne "ha-a."
A ne "i-hin."
A ne "ay si dira ni koira."
A ne "taari no.
970 Ay wo weyboro man bey ga duma
ay banda
Ga loomi ay banda ce fo."
A haaru a ne,
"Ni mana ga jin ga ay fay,
Ay no ga jin ga ni fay."
975 A ne "a-a ni ga taari
Ni si ba dey ni ma dira no."
A ne "wallahi ay wo ga dira,
Amma ay ga jin ga ni fay.
Ni si ga bey no,
980 Ay jin ga ni fay.
Ay bana mo weyborey kul ka ni jin
ga zamba se."
Albora nda inga plan,
Dabari kul kan alboro ga wani
laala ra,
Weyboro wo nda alboro miila,
985 Inga gonad dabari wey
Weyboro wone follon ga ni compile.
A ne, "hal jirbi hinza,
I tacanta hane,
Manci ni bey handin no bor ga koy
ga ni fari guna

990 Ga di buzugu?"
A ne "ma koy ni fari handin."
A ne "ni ga bey kan ay ga jin ga ni
fay."
Koweyo na inga jinayey sambu ga
dira.
Jirbi hinza hane borkul ga koy
inga Fari.
995 Ko aro koy inga fari
Manci bone!
A goro ga barey.
Hangasiney buzugo go no ga fara-
rara ga koy.
Boro mo nda fonney kal nessa,
A ma di busugo go ga gussam
nangu follon.
1000 Sohon ne hare sinda haykul.
To boroo hinka din no,
I ne to lalle soon ya weybora
1005 Zama a ga wande fay.
Boro fay yagga
Boro fay ahakku
I ne to lalle sohon ya weybora
hagu a se.
Weybora ga kurhye yaaga fay,
1010 Albora fay wande hakku
To ni di yagga koyo din na combile
Zama a wani dabari nda.
A se no I na kakawo te.
I ne wallahi alboro wo haykul kan
a te,
1015 Weyboro wo waani plan nda.
Alboro wo ize futu tarey,
Nda haykul kan ni ga te laala ra,
Tu kul kan weyboro waana nda nin.
Zama dabari boobo no a se.

**Oh, young girls, if you know God
(Susan Rasmussen)**

1. Kaye tchibararene kontassamat yala
2. Arghimat addal, addal yoholame
3. Azel iguequou fel yighiwen
4. Yinad ikhdam nene atawra

5. Tatigat degh Niger, winad iganene
6. Ejina in temse wan d'eneg aloq
7. Yighwen sanounki [Hausa term] wene
   ilingatnene
8. Iss Jaran
9. Nikou inighawene
10. Tchihoulene yighwan Mahamane
11. Entene Kadi, Al Mustapha, Ali,
12. Kamat, ighre Ganene, yissisbssa
    eguime.

Song for the Women of Nigeria
(Beverly Mack)

1   Allah namu, ma'aikin Allah namu,
    Taimaka matan Nijeriya,
    Allah namu ma'aikin Allah namu,
    Tagaza matan Nijeriya,
5   Matan Nijeriya,
    Matan Nijeriya,
    Kowane aiki za ku yi
    Matan Nijeriya,
    Matan Nijeriya,
10 Kui 'ko'kari ku gane,
    Kowane aiki ku iya,
    Ina baken ofis mata, ofis kun iya
    Matan Nijeriya, kowane aiki za
       ku yi,
    A ba ku ri'kon ma ku ri'ke
15 Aikin ofis kun iya,
    Ministoci ma kun iya,
    A ba ku ri'kon ma ku ri'ke 'ko'kari
       matan Nijeriya,
    Taftoci ma duka kun iya,
    Ka gani maza 'yan Nijeria
20 Matan Nijeriya kowane aiki ku iya,
    Kowane aiki ku iya,
    Matan Nijeriya, kowane aiki
       ku iya,
    Matan Nijeriya, ofis, zaman ofis
       ku iya,
    Takarda kun iya
25 Takarda kun iya

Matan Nijeriya, ri'kon makaranta
   ku iya,
Matan Nijeriya, ri'kon makaranta
   ku ri'ke,
Ministoci ma ku iya,
Matan Nijeriya, kowane aiki ku iya,
30 Kowane aiki ku iya,
   Nan matan Nijeriya, taftoci ma
      ku iya,
   Taftoci ku iya,
   Matan Nijeriya kowane aiki ku iya,
   Wace yanga za su yi?
35 Wace yanga za su yi?
   Takarda ma duka kun iya,
   Zaman ofis ma kun iya,
   Ri'kon biro ma kun iya,
   Kowace yanga za su yi?
40 Maza wace yanga za su yi?
   Matan Nijeriya
   A ba ku mi'kon ma ku ri'ke
   Matan Nijeriya, a ba ku mi'kon ma
      ku ri'ke
   Zaman mulki ma kun iya,
45 Matan Nijeriya,
   Takarda kun iya,
   Tafureta ma duka kun iya,
   Matan Nijeriya,
   Tafureta ma duka kun iya,
50 Matan Nijeriya,
   Kowace yanga za ku yi?
   Maza wace yanga za ku yi?
   Zaman ofis ma sun iya,
   A ba su kujera su ri'ke
55 A ba su kujera su ri'ke
   Matan Nijeriya,
   A ba ku kujera ku ri'ke,
   Matan Nijeriya,
   Kowane aiki ku iya,
60 Tukin mota kun iya, tukin jirgi
      kun iya,
   Jirgin sama ma duka kun iya,
   Jirgin sama ma duka kun iya,
   Matan Nijeriya

Godiya matan Nijeriya, sun biya
    mu mun gode masu,
65 Godiya matan Nijeriya, sun biya
    mu mun gode masu,
Alo, 'yan Nijeriya,
Alo, 'yan Nijeriya
Godiya ta 'yan Nijeriya,
Alo, 'yan Nijeriya, kowane aiki
    ku iya
70 Kowane aiki ku iya, kuma kowane
    aiki kun sani,
Rubutu takarda kun iya, bugun
    tafureta kun iya,
Jirgin sama ma duka kun iya,
Zaman ofis ma kun sani
Aikin doka ku iya,
75 Kuma 'dan sanda ma ku iya,
Aikin kostam ku iya,
Am mi'ka maku lalle ku ri'ke,
Matan Nijeriya,
Matan Nijeriya, kowane aiki ku sani,
80 Kowane aiki ku iya,
Kuma kowane aiki ku iya,
Ko Allah ya sani, matan Nijeriya,
Biyayya kun iya,
Soyayya kun iya, da biyayya 'yan
    Nijeriya,
85 Soyayya kun iya, da biyayya kun iya,
A gaya muku can Nijeriya,
Godiya sa albarka mun yaba
A gaya muku 'yan Nijeriya, godiya
sa albarka mun yaba.

**Yande the Wrestler
(Luciana Penna-Diaw)**

Singer
Yànde mbëro, mbëro yaay daan,
Yànde mbëro, mbëro yaay daan.

Chorus
Yànde mbëro, mbëro yaay daan,
Yànde mbëro, mbëro yaay daan,
Yànde mbëro, mbëro yaay daan,

Yànde mbëro, mbëro yaay daan,
Yànde mbëro, mbëro yaay daan,
Yànde mbëro, mbëro yaay daan,
Yànde mbëro, mbëro yaay daan,
Yànde mbëro, mbëro yaay daan.

Singer
Mbëro, sunu mbër mi ngembuna,
Yànde mbëro, mbëro yaay daan.

Chorus
Mbëro, sunu mbër mi ngembuna,
Yànde mbëro, mbëro yaay daan.
Yànde mbëro, mbëro yaay daan.
Yànde mbëro, mbëro yaay daan.

Singer
Mbëro, sunu mbër mi ngembuna,
Yànde mbëro, mbëro yaay daan.

Wrestle Men (George Joseph)

1. *Debbe*
Bëreleen góor ñi,
Gaa ñi bëreleen,
Làmb bu ca góor nekkul
Jigéen a koy moom.

2. *Awu*
Bëreleen góor ñi,
Góor ñi bëreleen,
Làmb bu ca góor nekkul
Jigéen a koy moom.

3. *Debbe*
Bëreleen góor ñi,
Góor ñi bëreleen,
Làmb bu ca góor nekkul
Jigéen a koy moom.

4. *Awu*
Bëreleen góor ñi,
Góor ñi bëreleen,
Làmb bu ca góor nekkul
Jigéen a koy moom.

5. *Debbe*
Mànjaago baa nga daanu ca pom ba

Diw ga jalaañoo
Lànk naa duma bëreek mànjaago
Aayee!
Làmb bu ca góor nekkul
Jigéen a koy moom.

6. *Awu*
Bëreleen góor ñi,
Góor ñi bëreleen,
Làmb bu ca góor nekkul
Jigéen a koy moom.

7. *Debbe*
Mànjaago baa nga daanu ca pom ba
Diw ga jalaañoo
Lànk naa duma bëreek mànjaago
Aayee!
Làmb bu ca góor nekkul
Jigéen a koy moom.

8. *Awu*
Bëreleen góor ñi,
Góor ñi bëreleen,
Làmb bu ca góor nekkul
Jigéen a koy moom.

9. *Debbe*
Mànjaago baa nga daanu ca pom ba
Diw ga jalaañoo
Lànk naa duma bëreek mànjaago
Aayee!
Làmb bu ca góor nekkul
Jigéen a koy moom.

10. *Awu*
Bëreleen góor ñi,
Góor ñi bëreleen,
Làmb bu ca góor nekkul
Jigéen a koy moom.

11. *Debbe*
Bëreleen góor ñi,
Góor ñi bëreleen,
Làmb bu ca góor nekkul
Jigéen a koy moom.

12. *Awu*
Bëreleen góor ñi,

Góor ñi bëreleen,
Làmb bu ca góor nekkul
Jigéen a koy moom.

13. *Debbe*
Billaay mànjaago baa nga daanu ca pom ba
Diw ga jalaañoo
Lànk naa duma bëreek mànjaago
Aayee!
Làmb bu ca góor nekkul
Jigéen a koy moom.

Give to the griot (Marloes Janson)

Jaloo n so
N batufaa n so
Yee jaloo n so
N batufaa n so
Jaloo n so
N batufaa n so
Foro musu jawoolu turuti marati
Wolu keng na jaloo
te keme soto jali abadaa
Jaloo n so
N batufaa n so
Ning i ye jaloo bali wo
Ala si i bali
Jaloo n so
N batufaa n so
Ning i ye jaloo so
Ala si i so feng na
Jaloo n so
N batufaa n so
N ko i la jaloo so
Tubaaboo n so

Jaloo n so
N batufaa n so
Foro musu jawoolu turuti marati
Wolu keng na jaloo
Jaloo n so
N batufaa n so
Ning i ye jaloo bali
Ala si i bali
Jaloo n so

N batufaa n so
Ning i ye jaloo so
Ala si i so feng na
Jaloo n so
N batufaa n so
Ning i ye jaloo bali
Ala si i bali

Jaloo n so
N batufaa n so
Foro musu jawoolu turuti marati
Wolu keng na jaloo
te keme soto jali abadaa
Jaloo n so
N batufaa n so
N ko i la jaloo so
N batufaa n so.

Father and mother of the poor people
(Thomas A. Hale and Aissata Niandou)

Talkay nya da i baabe
Nyalawayay kurnye

Kan da asi kwayre si kaanu
Da a si mo a si bine kaanu
A ma nyalay dake
Fofo mayga
Kan da a si kwayre si kaanu
Da a si mo a si bine kaanu
Iri te se nya
Iri ta iri se baabe
Ma iri babba
Sunfuleyni
Ma te iri se ciiri kan iri ga dan iri hoyay la
Ma te iri se ji kan iri ga ta iri bita la
Ma te iri se kaayi da mudun
Hala iri ma bontabay karu
Nga no iri ga jinde jaru da koyzo kan ka
Hala a ma iri babba koyzo kan ka
Hala a ma iri nwayende koyzo kan ka
Kan ga tamu dan iri se
Nin ti iri moyay
Nin ti iri dijo
Nin ti iri ciya da iri kabey
Kan ga iri go ga dira.

Bibliography

Anonymous. *Itinéraires et contacts de cultures:* vol. 8, *Chansons d'Afrique et des Antilles.* Paris: L'Harmattan, 1988, pp. 21–28, 51–52.

Bâ, Amadou Hampaté. *The Fortunes of Wangrin.* Bloomington: Indiana University Press, 1999.

Ba, Birahim Ciré. "La vie de l'AOF et l'Ecole." *Bulletin d'Enseignement de l'Afrique Occidentale Française,* no. 71 (Jan.–Mar. 1930).

Barber, Karin. *I Could Speak till Tomorrow: Oriki, Women, and the Past in a Yoruba Town.* Edinburgh: Edinburgh University Press, 1991.

Belvaude, Catherine. *Ouverture sur la littérature en Mauritanie.* Paris: L'Harmattan, 1989.

Bender, Wolfgang. *Sweet Mother: Modern African Music.* Chicago: University of Chicago Press, 1991.

Bird, Charles. "Sara." In John William Johnson, Thomas A. Hale, and Stephen Belcher, eds., *Oral Epics from Africa: Vibrant Voices from a Vast Continent.* Bloomington: Indiana University Press, 1997, pp. 114–123.

Bisilliat, Jeanne, and Dioulé Laya. *Les zamu; ou, poèmes sur les noms.* Niamey, Niger: Centre National de la Recherche Scientifique et Technique de la République du Niger, 1972.

Bourgault, Louise M. *Playing for Life: Performance in Africa in the Age of AIDS.* Durham, N.C.: Carolina Academic, 2003.

———. "Youth Culture, Peer Education, and a New Generation of *Jelimusow* in Mali: Women's AIDS Songs in Context." Paper presented at the Princeton Conference on Women's Songs from West Africa, May 2–4, 2003.

Boyd, Raymond, and Richard Fardon. "Bìsíwééri: The Songs and Times of a Muslim Chamba Woman." *African Languages and Cultures* 5(1) (1992): 11–41.

Brévié, Jules. "A propos d'une chanson bambara." *Annuaire et mémoires du Comité d'Etudes Historiques et Scientifiques de l'Afrique Occidentale Française* 1917 (1918): 217–222.

Caillé, René. *Journal d'un voyage à Tombouctou.* 1830. Paris: La Découverte, 1989.

Calame-Griaule, Geneviève. *Contes tendres, contes cruels du Sahel nigérien.* Paris: Gallimard, 2002.

Camara, Brahim, and Jan Jansen. "Do Griottes Recite Epics? The Case of Siramori Diabaté (Mali)." Paper contributed to the Women's Songs in West Africa project.

Camara, Sory. *Vergers de l'aube*. Bordeaux, France: Confluences, 2001.

Cazenave, Odile. *Femmes Rebelles: Naissance d'un nouveau roman africain au féminin*. Paris: L'Harmattan, 1996 [*Rebellious Women: The New Generation of Female African Novelists*. Translated by the author. Boulder, Colo.: Lynne Rienner, 2000].

Couloubaly, Pascal Baba F. *Une société rurale bambara à travers des chants de femmes*. Dakar, Senegal: Institut Fondamental d'Afrique Noire, 1990.

d'Almeida, Irène Assiba. *Francophone Women Writers: Destroying the Emptiness of Silence*. Gainesville: University Press of Florida, 1994.

Deluz, Ariane. "Féminin nocturne." In Ariane Deluz, Colette Le Cour Grandmaison, and Anne Retel-Laurenti, eds., *Vies et paroles de femmes africaines*. Paris: Karthala, 2001, pp. 157–206.

———. "Women's Songs from the Guro of Côte d'Ivoire." Paper presented at the Princeton Conference on Women's Songs from West Africa, May 2–4, 2003.

Derive, Jean. "Le fonctionnement sociologique de la littérature orale: L'exemple du Dioula de Kong (Côte d'Ivoire)." Diss., University of Paris III, 1986.

Diagana, Ousmane Moussa. *Chants traditionnels du pays soninké*. Paris: L'Harmattan, 1990.

Diakité, Bah. "Bambara Women's Songs and Their Socio-Cultural Contexts in Southern Mali." Paper presented at the Princeton Conference on Women's Songs from West Africa, May 2–4, 2003.

Diarra, Fatoumata-Agnès. *Femmes africaines en devenir*. Paris: Anthropos, 1971.

Diawara, Mamadou. *La Graine de la parole*. Stuttgart: Studien zur Kulturkunde, 1990.

———. "Le Griot Mande à l'heure de la globalisation." *Cahiers d'études africaines* 144(25) (1966): 591–612.

Dione, Salif. *L'Education traditionelle à travers les chants et les poèmes Seereer*. Dakar, Senegal: University of Dakar Press, 1983.

Durán, Lucy. "Birds of Mande: The Women Singers of Wassoulou." Paper presented at the Mande Studies Association Conference, Leiden, Mar. 21, 1995.

———. "Birds of Wasulu: Freedom of Expression and Expressions of Freedom in the Popular Music of Southern Mali." *British Journal of Ethnomusicology* 4 (1995): 101–134.

———. "Djely Mousso—Women of Mali." *Folk Roots* 75 (Sept. 1989): 34–39.

———. "Jelimusow: The Superwomen of Malian Music." In Graham Furniss and Liz Gunner, eds., *Power, Marginality and African Oral Literature*. Cambridge: Cambridge University Press, 1995.

———. "Mali/Guinea—Mande Music: West Africa's Musical Powerhouse." In Simon Broughton, Mark Ellingham, and Richard Trillo, eds., *World Music: The Rough Guide*: vol. 1, *Africa, Europe and the Middle East*. London: Rough Guides, 1999.

———. "'Musical Bargaining': Recordings and Musical Creativity in the Mande Jeli Tradition." Paper presented at the Thirty-Eighth African Studies Association Annual Conference, Orlando, Florida, Nov. 4, 1995.

———. "Music Created by God." In Simon Broughton, Mark Ellingham, David Muddyman, and Richard Trillo, eds., *World Music: The Rough Guide*. London: Rough Guides, 1994.

———. "Savannah Sex Wars." *Wire Magazine* 114 (Aug. 1993): 42–44.

———. "Stars and Songbirds: Mande Female Singers in Urban Music, Mali 1980–1999." Diss., University of London, 1999.

———. "Women, Music, and the 'Mystique' of Hunters in Mali." In Ingrid Monsoon, ed., *The African Diaspora: A Musical Perspective*. New York: Garland, 2000.

Es-Sa'di, Abderraman. *Tarikh es-Sudan*. Translated by Octave Houdas. 1898–1900. 2nd ed., Paris: Adrien-Maisonneuve, 1964.

Fadiga, Bouillagui. "Une circoncision chez les Markas de Soudan." *Bulletin du Comité d'Études Historiques et Scientifiques d'Afrique Occidentale Française* 18(4) (Oct.–Dec. 1934): 565–577.

Foster, Jack. *Love Songs of the New Kingdom*. Austin: University of Texas Press, 1974.

Furniss, Graham. "Hausa Poetry on the Nigerian Civil War." *African Languages and Cultures* 4(1) (1991): 21–28.

———. *Orality: The Power of the Spoken Word*. New York: Palgrave Macmillan, 2004.

Furniss, Graham, ed. *Poetry, Prose and Popular Culture in Hausa*. Edinburgh: Edinburgh University Press, 1996.

Ganay, Solange de. *Le sanctuaire Kama Blon de Kangaba*. Paris: Editions Nouvelles du Sud, 1995.

Gueye, Marame. "Wolof Wedding Songs from Senegal." Paper presented at the Princeton Conference on Women's Songs from West Africa, May 2–4, 2003.

Guignard, Michel. *Musique, honneur et plaisir au Sahara*. Paris: Librairie Orientaliste Paul Geuthner, 1975.

Hale, Thomas A. *Griots and Griottes: Masters of Words and Music*. Bloomington: Indiana University Press, 1998.

———. *Griottes of the Sahel: Female Keepers of the Songhay Oral Tradition in Niger*. Video. Pennsylvania State University, 1990.

———. Songhay interviews and songs recorded in Niger. Unpublished, 1989.

———. "Voices from the Past: Documentary Traces of Women Singers and Songs from the Sahel, 1352–1915." Paper presented at the Princeton Conference on Women's Songs from West Africa, May 2–4, 2003.

Hale, Thomas A., and Paul Stoller. "Oral Art, Society, and Survival in the Sahel Zone." In Stephen Arnold, ed., *African Literature Studies: The Present State/L'Etat présent*. Washington, D.C.: Three Continents, 1985.

Hama, Boubou. *L'Essence du verbe*. Niamey, Niger: Centre d'Études Historiques et Linguistiques par Tradition Orale, 1986.

Hamdun, Said, and Noel King. *Ibn Battuta in Black Africa*. London: Rex Collings, 1975.

Harris, Laura Arnston. "The Play of Ambiguity in Praise-Song Performance." Diss., Indiana University, 1992.

Hoffman, Barbara G. *Griots at War: Conflict, Conciliation, and Caste in Mande*. Bloomington: Indiana University Press, 2000.

Hunter, L., and C. E. Ousmarou. *Aspects of the Aesthetics of Hausa Verbal Art*. Cologne: Koppe, 2001.

Hunwick, John. *Timbuktu and the Songhay Empire: Al-Sadi's Tarikh al-Sudan Down to 1613 and Other Contemporary Documents*. Leiden: Brill, 1999.

Ibrahim, Mohammed Sani. "Kowa ya sha kida, abinsa ya bayar: Nazari kan wakokin makadan sarauta da makadan jama'a." 1976. In Graham Furniss, ed., *Poetry, Prose and Popular Culture in Hausa*. Edinburgh: Edinburgh University Press, 1996, pp. 146–147.

Jansen, Jan. *Siramuri Diabate et ses enfants*. Utrecht: ISOR; and Bamako: Institut des Sciences Humaines, 1991.

Janson, Marloes. *The Best Hand Is the Hand That Always Gives: Griottes and Their Profession in Eastern Gambia.* Leiden: CNWS, 2002.

———. "Griottes, Songs and Rewards." Paper presented at the Forty-Third Annual Meeting of the African Studies Association, Nashville, Tennessee, Nov. 16–19, 2000.

———. "Research in Transit." Paper presented at the Fifth International Conference on Mande Studies, Leiden, June 17–21, 2002.

———. "Words in Context: Performances by Griottes in the Gambia." Paper presented at the Princeton Conference on Women's Songs from West Africa, May 2–4, 2003.

Jewsiewicki, Bogumil. "African Historical Studies: Academic Knowledge as 'Usable Past,' and Radical Scholarship." Paper presented at the Thirtieth Annual Meeting of the African Studies Association, Denver, Colorado, Dec. 19–23, 1987.

Joseph, George. "Anesthetic for Pain: Women's Tattooing Songs from Kajoor." Paper presented at the Princeton Conference on Women's Songs from West Africa, May 2–4, 2003.

———. Wolof songs and interviews recorded in Senegal. Unpublished, 2002.

Kaboré, Oger. *Les oiseaux s'ébattent: Chansons enfantines au Burkina-Faso.* Paris: L'Harmattan, 1993.

Kane, Cheikh Hamidou. *Ambiguous Adventure.* London: Heinemann, 1972. Translated by Katherine Woods. [*L'Aventure ambiguë.* Paris: Juillard, 1961].

Kane, Issa. "L'Enfant Toucouleur." *Bulletin d'Enseignement de l'Afrique Occidentale Française* 79 (Apr.–June 1932): 99.

Kâti, Mahmoud. *Tarîkh el-Fettâch.* Translated by Octave Houdas and Maurice Delafosse. 1913. Paris: Maisonneuve, 1981.

Katy, Charles. *Chants de femmes seereer.* Dakar-Étoile, Senegal: Prometra International, 2003a.

———. "Pantheistic Symbols in Seereer Women's Songs." Paper presented at the Princeton Conference on Women's Songs from West Africa, May 2–4, 2003b.

Keita, Abdoulaye. "Approche ethnolinguistique de la tradition orale Wolof (Contes et Taasu)." Master's thesis, University of Dakar, 1986.

Kesteloot, Lilyan, and Bassirou Dieng. *Les épopées d'Afrique noire.* Paris: Karthala, 1997.

Kouyate, Tata Bambo. *Jatigui.* London: Ace Records, 1989.

La Courbe, Michel Jajolet de. *Premier voyage du Sieur de La Courbe fait à la Coste d'Afrique en 1685.* Edited by Pierre Cultru. Paris: Champion, 1913.

Langeveld, Kirsten. "The Dynamics of Lyrics in Jola Kanyalen Songs from the Casamance Region of Senegal: From Tradition to Globalization." Paper presented at the Princeton Conference on Women's Songs from West Africa, May 2–4, 2003.

LeBrun, R. P. "Un marriage khassonké." *Bulletin du Comité d'Études Historiques et Scientifiques d'Afrique Occidentale Française* 18(4) (1934): 672–682.

Leymarie, Isabelle. *Les Griots Wolof du Sénégal.* Paris: Servédit/Maisonneuve et Larose, 1999.

Luneau, René. "Chansons d'excision Bambara." In Anon., *Recueil de Littérature Manding.* Paris: Agence de Coopération Culturelle et Technique, 1980, pp. 54–65.

———. *Chants de femmes au Mali.* Paris: Luneau-Ascot, 1981. Reprint, Paris: Karthala, 2010.

———. "Les Chemins de la Noce." Diss., University of Paris, 1974.

Mack, Beverly B. "Muslim Hausa Women's Songs." Paper presented at the Princeton Conference on Women's Songs from West Africa, May 2–4, 2003.

———. *Muslim Women Sing: Hausa Popular Song.* Bloomington: Indiana University Press, 2004.

Mack, Beverly, and Jean Boyd. *One Woman's Jihad: Nana Asmaù, Scholar and Scribe.* Bloomington: Indiana University Press, 2000.

Maikafi, Shekarau Umar. "Nazari akan wakokin matan Hausawa ne gargajiya." B.A. final paper, Bayero University, 1977.

Mamadi, Kaba. *Anthologie de chants mandingues.* Paris: L'Harmattan, 1995.

Manniche, Lisa. *Music and Musicians in Ancient Egypt.* London: British Museum Press, 1991.

Mashi, Musa Barah. "Gudunmawar Hajiya Barmani Choge mai Amada ga adabin Hawsa." B.A. final paper, Bayero University, 1982.

Mbengue, Mariama Ndoye. "Introduction à la literature orale léboue: Analyse sociologique et expression littéraire." Diss., University of Dakar, 1981.

McNee, Lisa. "The Black and the White: Race and Oral Poetry in Mauritania." In Christopher Wise, ed., *The Desert Shore: Literatures of the Sahel.* Boulder, Colo.: Lynne Rienner, 2001.

———. *Selfish Gifts: Senegalese Women's Autobiographical Discourses.* Albany: State University of New York Press, 2000.

Mécheri-Saada, Nadia. *Musique touarégue de l'Ahaggar.* Paris: L'Harmattan, 1994.

Modic, Kate E. "Song, Performance and Power: The Bèn Ka Di Women's Association in Bamako, Mali." Diss., Indiana University, 1996.

Mounkaïla, Fatima. "Poetry from Inside, Poetry from Outside: Sayings about Names of Songhay-Zarma Women in Niger." Paper presented at the Princeton Conference on Women's Songs from West Africa, May 2–4, 2003.

Muurling, Nienke. "'People with Money and People without Money Are Not the Same': Income and Distribution Strategies of a *Jelimuso* between Mali and France." Paper presented at the Princeton Conference on Women's Songs from West Africa, May 2–4, 2003.

Namaiwa, Boubé. "The Social and Historical Meaning of Some Azna Deities in the Songs of Taguimba Bouzou." Paper presented at the Princeton Conference on Women's Songs from West Africa, May 2–4, 2003.

Ndongo, Siré Mamadou. *Le Fantang: Poèmes mythiques des bergers peuls.* Paris: UNESCO, 1986.

Niandou, Aissata. "Deconstructing the Stereotypes of the Passive and Voiceless African Women." Paper presented at the Princeton Conference on Women's Songs from West Africa, May 2–4, 2003.

Niane, Djibril Tamsir. *Sundiata: An Epic of Old Mali.* Translated by G. D. Pickett. London: Longman, 1965 [*Soundjata; ou, L'Épopée mandingue.* Paris: Présence Africaine, 1960].

Nnaemeka, Obioma. *Feminisms, Sisterhood and Power: From Africa to the Diaspora.* Trenton, N.J.: World Press, 1998.

Norris, H. T. *Shinqiti Folk Literature and Song.* Oxford: Oxford University Press, 1968.

Oger, Kabore. *Les oiseaux s'ébattent: Chanson enfantines au Burkina-Faso.* Paris: L'Harmattan, 1993.

Penna-Diaw, Luciana. "Regional Similarities and Differences in Songs by Wolof Women." Paper presented at the Princeton Conference on Women's Songs from West Africa, May 2–4, 2003.

Perron, Michel. "Chants populaires de la Sénégambie et du Niger: Quelques observa-
    tions générales suivies de quelques chants inédits." *Bulletin de l'Agence Générale
    des Colonies* 206 (Oct. 1930): 803–811.
Rasmussen, Susan J. *The Poetics and Politics of Tuareg Aging.* DeKalb: Northern Illi-
    nois University Press, 1997.
———. "'What Is a Song?': Transformations in Tuareg Tende-Singing over Time and
    the Problem of Women's Voices and Local Feminisms." Paper presented at the
    Princeton Conference on Women's Songs from West Africa, May 2–4, 2003.
Sagna, El Hadji. "La Problématique de l'enfant dans la littérature traditionelle dioula:
    Contes, chants." Master's thesis, University of Dakar, 1986–1987.
Schulz, Dorothea E. *Perpetuating the Politics of Praise.* Cologne, Germany: Rüdiger
    Köppe, 2001.
Sembène, Ousmane. *Les bouts de bois de Dieu.* Paris: Le Livre Contemporain, 1960.
———. *God's Bits of Wood.* Garden City, N.Y.: Doubleday, 1962.
Sidibé, Mamby. "La famille chez les Foula de Birgo du Fouladougou Arbala et du
    Fouladougou Saboula." *Bulletin du Comité d'Études Historiques et Scientifiques
    d'Afrique Occidentale Française* 18(4) (Oct.–Dec. 1934): 462–539.
Sidikou, Aissata. *Recreating Words, Reshaping Worlds: The Verbal Art of Women from
    Niger, Mali, and Senegal.* Trenton, N.J.: Africa World Press, 2001.
———. "Space, Language and Identity in the Symbol of the Palm Tree." Paper pre-
    sented at the Princeton Conference on Women's Songs from West Africa, May
    2–4, 2003.
Stone, Ruth M. *Let the Inside Be Sweet.* Bloomington: Indiana University Press, 1982.
Street, Brian. *Literacy in Theory and Practice.* Cambridge: Cambridge University
    Press, 1984.
Tandia, Aliou Kissima. *Poésie orale soninké et éducation traditionnelle.* Dakar, Sene-
    gal: Nouvelles Editions Africaines du Sénégal, 1999.
Tauzin, Aline. *Figures du féminin dans la société maure (Mauritanie).* Paris: Karthala,
    2001.
———. "Saharan Music: About a Feminine Identity." Paper presented at the Princeton
    Conference on Women's Songs from West Africa, May 2–4, 2003.
Thiaw, Issa Laye. *La Femme seereer (Sénégal).* Paris: L'Harmattan, 2005.
Traoré, Mamadou. "Une danse curieuse: Le moribayasa." *Notes Africaines* 15 (July
    1942): 5–6.

Index

Tchôta, 106; Thiès, 10; Timbuktu, 5, 6, 27; Togo, 16; Tukolor empire, 20; Ungogo, 86; United States, 31; Waalo, 30; Wagadu, 28; West Indies, 22; Wolof, 4; Wudil, 86; Yaayeem, 110; Yadakunya, 86; Yatakala, 95–96; Yatenga, 25; Yogpeongo, 57; Yourid, 55; Zarma, 105; Zinder, 1

plant/plant products: acacia, 82; cacao, 16; calabash, 106; coffee, 16; cotton, 16; *gao*, 55–56; gourd, 82; grain, 107; indigo, 25; *jujube*, 75; *kokorbe*, 53; *kuubu*, 42; *nèrè*, 101; *nime*, 42; rice, 16; seeds, 63–64; shoots, 65, 82; straw, 108; *talhana*, 42; thorns, 108; yams, 16; *zemtaaba*, 56–57

planting, 63, 81; season, 81

plastic bags, 86

political criticism, 79

polygyny, 1, 4, 10, 49–50

postpartum depression, 69

potion, 51

powder, 108

power, 108

praise, 94

precious metals, 104

pregnancy, 68–69

president of Mauritania, 82

president of Senegal, 82

primitive, 12

prison, 106

Prophet, the, 87

protection, 110

qadi, 106

radio, 2, 33

railroad strike, 10–11

rain, 81–82

rainy season, 63–64

Rasmussen, Susan, xi, 84

rawhide, 90

real estate, 20, 29

rebellion, 84

rebels, 79; female, 84

reins, 102

rejection, 10

relatives, 9, 68, 70, 76, 93, 105; aunt, 45, 72; brother, 8, 46, 55, 107; brother-in-law, 8, 45–47, 62, 68; daughter, 55, 60, 76, 88, 94, 106; eldest son, 57; father, 54, 48–49, 60, 62–63, 96, 105, 109; father-in-law, 46, 55; grandfather, 73; grandmother, 72, 82, 101; grandparents, 49; half-brother, 71; mother, 45–47, 49, 53, 60–62, 64, 68, 70–72, 76, 78–79, 94, 96, 101, 104, 105–106, 115–116, ; mother-daughter tie, 8, 46–47, 55, 76; mother-in-law, 107; older brother, 57; parents, 55, 59, 68, 75; siblings, 55; sister, 46, 49, 72, 80–81, 107; sister-in-law, 8, 55, 104; son, 80; uncle, 49

religion, xi

reproach, 108

revenge, 65

rewards, 8, 83, 95–96

ridge beam, 106

ritual. *See* ceremonies/rituals

rope, 40

Rosenberg, Aaron, xii

ruby, 103

ruler, 95

Sa Ndiouki, 73

Saadu, 43

Sagado, Gitu, 95

Sagna, El Hadji, 78

sales, 58

Salimata, 54

Samba, 78–79

Sanana, 78

sanctuary, 110

sankira, 50

Sara, 39

Sarraounia Mangou, 25

school, 75

Schulze, Dorothea, 96

sea, 20, 103

sedentary, 29

Sega, Demba, 19–20

self-esteem, 108

Sembène, Ousmane, 10, 39